THE LOUIS VUITTON CUP 25 YEARS OF YACHT RACING IN PURSUIT OF THE AMERICA'S CUP

THE LOUIS VUITTON CUP 25 YEARS OF YACHT RACING IN PURSUIT OF THE AMERICA'S CUP

Edited and preface
by Bruno Troublé
Text and drawings by François Chevalier
Translated from the French by Krister Swartz

ABRAMS,
NEW YORK

François Chevalier gives special thanks to Jacques Taglang.

Design: www.be-poles.com
Photo research: Anne Mensior

English-Language Edition:
Magali Veillon, Project Manager
Miranda Ottewell, Editor
Shawn Dahl, Designer
Jules Thomson, Production Manager

Library of Congress Cataloging-in-Publication Data

Chevalier, Francois, 1944–
The Louis Vuitton Cup : 25 years of yacht racing in pursuit of the America's Cup / by Francois Chevalier.
p. cm.
ISBN 978-0-8109-7114-1
1. Louis Vuitton Cup—History. 2. America's Cup—History.
3. Yacht racing—History. I. Title.
GV829.C484 2008
797.124'6–dc22
2008027922

Published in 2008 by Abrams, an imprint of Harry N. Abrams, Inc.

Printed and bound in France
10 9 8 7 6 5 4 3 2 1

HNA
harry n. abrams, inc.
a subsidiary of La Martinière Groupe
115 West 18th Street
New York, NY 10011
www.hnabooks.com

Cover photograph © Bob Grieser

CONTENTS

Preface

BRUNO TROUBLÉ

The Inexhaustible Passion for a Venerable Trophy

I am often asked why I have tirelessly dedicated a very large part of my life to the America's Cup.

Is it out of frustration at not having won?

Without a doubt. France, the world leader in leisure and ocean sailing, has had the means to win, many times. When I accidentally nick myself shaving with a Bic razor, I imagine that Baron Bich is still taking revenge for our loss in 1980, one of the years when victory seemed within our reach.

Because of the rich history of the trophy?

Visit the New York Yacht Club and you will understand the unique character of this event, which extends in its significance well beyond the domain of sports. The Cup is a witness to more than one hundred and fifty years of geopolitical change in the Western world, and to the emergence of the Pacific arena as a vital power. Faced with these young, brash bankers of New York, products of a colony of the British Empire, who defied—and triumphed over—the era's world masters in 1851; with Australia triumphing over the West in 1983; with the upstart New Zealanders in 1995, history has stammered. . . .

Each time a small country, without any special technology, came to dominate Goliath by the force of its will and its determination to bring down mountains. The Swiss victory and China's presence in the 2007 Louis Vuitton Cup are not contradictions. This is the fruit of the globalized climate, as the world opens up. For the first time, on some crews, few or no team members are natives of the countries they represent.

The human element?

More than any other sport, the Cup has created and attracted exceptional personalities. This was true in the nineteenth century, and it is still so today. It is pointless to name names here; they appear on every page of this book. They are there for the glory at hand, for national pride, but also for the struggle: "I went because it was impossible to win" is the motto of all the captains. Fascinating.

Its exclusive character?

...Elitist, some might say. For a long time considered a dream and a summer pastime for millionaires, the Cup has retained its exclusive character. It is reassuring that—faced with the competition of the great popular sports—an event on such a small scale can retain its worldwide audience.

Louis Vuitton has been the guardian of the temple for twenty-five years, and if the Cup has been able to conserve its exclusive character—of competitors and sponsors of great quality—while largely increasing its audience, it is because of Vuitton, which, in a certain fashion, has protected it. The importance of Louis Vuitton's partnership with the Cup has been obvious to me from day one.

No event in the world today is as appealing in its rich history—I am always learning new stories—in its avant-garde technology, and at the same time in its media coverage.

The America's Cup is the result of a very delicate alchemy. But in spite of its recent upheavals, it is still much bigger than the apprentice sorcerers who play with it, and it always recovers from the tempest to return to its original honor. It has always had a mad charm! When one loves a woman, can one always explain why?

Thanks to François Chevalier for having added to my unbridled enthusiasm a historian's discipline and precision, and an expert attention to detail.

1851
1980

Though defeated at every attempt for 132 years,
the challenger was sometimes a genuine threat. (Preceding spread) In 1967, *Gretel* passed *Weatherly* a few nautical miles from the finish line thanks to a fast start during the second regatta.
Photograph by Morris Rosenfeld (Mystic Seaport, Mystic, Connecticut)

The start of this 1920 race has much in common
with recent Louis Vuitton Cup regattas—two opponents, (above) the challenger *Shamrock IV* and *Resolute,* circling toward each other as people aboard a committee boat and a spectator boat looked on. Only a bottle of champagne is missing beside the passionate amateurs and elegant women on deck!
Photograph by Edwin Levick (The Mariners' Museum, Newport News, Virginia)

Chapter 1

The Birth of Two Legends: Louis Vuitton and the America's Cup

Halfway through the nineteenth century, the Industrial Revolution was under way. Under the aegis of liberal capitalism, Europe created a new framework, entrusting the destiny of humanity to machines. Modern steam engines and the spectacular expansion of the railways brought the continents closer together. After centuries of protectionism and isolation, the world discovered the virtues of free trade—an English invention. The driving force of this new economy, money, henceforth omnipresent, was circulated, borrowed, and invested in the stock market. Considerable fortunes were amassed and lost. This brashly confident, conquering society took progress as its religion, with the World Fairs acting as its new temples.

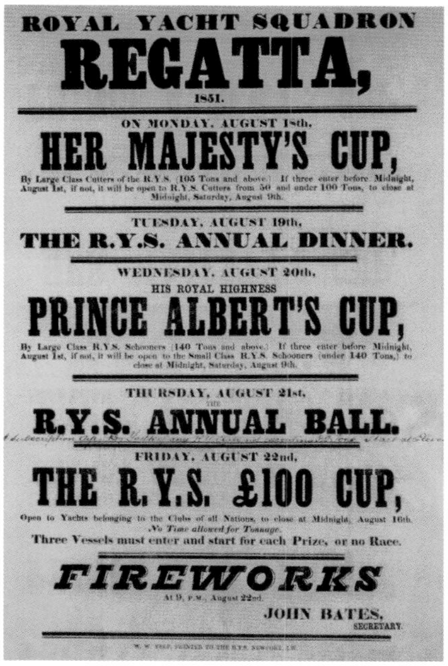

The race held on August 22, 1851, "open to yachts belonging to clubs of all nations," was the last of the RYS's Royal Regatta Week.
Archives Louis Vuitton/Media Center

Prince Albert's Great Exhibition of London in 1851, the first of its kind, gave participating nations an occasion to show advances and know-how in all fields. The modern competitive spirit of the Great Exhibition found an echo in the origin of the oldest trophy in contemporary sports: the America's Cup.

On the occasion of the London exhibition, an acquaintance of John Cox Stevens, president and founder of the New York Yacht Club (NYYC), steamship owner, and iron magnate, asked him to send a sailboat to represent the naval construction of the New World. Along with five friends, he commissioned the schooner *America.* From the outset, the project was a study in excellence: one clause stipulated that the yacht would not be paid for unless it was confirmed to be the fastest in the United States.

On its arrival in the Solent, the sound that separates the Isle of Wight from England, the schooner impressed everyone, but the press insisted that an English yacht club, the Royal Yacht Squadron (RYS), challenge it in a race around the Isle of Wight on August 22, 1851. Already the media was creating the history of the cup, inventing for the occasion this little dialogue with the English monarch, recounted in a speech by John Cox Stevens on his return from England:

"Who came first?"

"The *America.*"

"Who came second?"

"Ah! Your Majesty, there is no second!"

The legend of the America's Cup was born.

At the finish of the race around the Isle of Wight, the commodore of the Royal Yacht Squadron, the Earl of Wilton, presented Stevens with the One Hundred Guinea

Cup—the future America's Cup. Queen Victoria personally asked to visit the sailboat that beat the English fleet, sealing the indisputable superiority of the Americans. For 132 years, the victory remained with America, at the NYYC.

This unexpected American victory sparked the interest of an aristocracy and a bourgeoisie keen on new distractions and new honors. The new rich were hungry for modern leisure activities as much as for the luxury objects made available by modern industry and transportation. Traveling was in vogue, so it was natural that fine luggage should be developed; Louis Vuitton captured that spirit. The young artisan luggage-maker, supplying Empress Eugénie among others, opened his first Parisian boutique in 1854 on the rue Neuve-des-Capucines. The refined, lightweight trunk he created—a wooden frame covered in fabric, much lighter than leather—could be as easily stacked on the rear seat of an automobile as in the hold of an ocean liner. His wardrobe-trunk, a sort of mobile dressing room, was soon all the rage in steamship cabins. Lightness, sturdiness, functionality, elegance: Adapted to the modern lifestyle, luxury objects became the badges of the members of business and finance circles.

THEN EDWARD BURGESS CAME UP WITH A NEW YACHT DESIGN, A PERFECT BALANCE BETWEEN THE WIDE, SHALLOW YANKEE SLOOP AND THE DEEP, NARROW BRITISH CUTTER. HIS "COMPROMISE SLOOP," THE *PURITAN,* WON IN 1885.

The years passed and only in 1870 did the Englishman John Ashbury launch a new challenge, the *Cambria,* which lost to the fourteen best schooners of the NYYC. All of New York was on the water to watch these regattas; even Wall Street closed its trading floor. Ashbury tried again without success in 1871 with the *Livonia,* a schooner especially constructed for the event, in the first one-on-one match race, which would become the standard format for yachting.

After a weak attempt by Canadian Alexander Cuthbert to pit *Countess of Dufferin* against the schooner *Madeleine* in 1876, the Americans developed for the first time, five years later, a selection process to choose their defender. Joseph R. Busk's *Mischief,* which had been especially constructed for this defense, was selected after the 1881 elimination trials. Then Edward Burgess came up with a new yacht design, a perfect balance between the wide, shallow Yankee sloop and the deep, narrow British cutter. His "compromise sloop," the *Puritan,* won in 1885. He returned with the *Mayflower* and the *Volunteer* in 1886 and 1887.

For the America's Cup of 1893, naval architect Nathanael Herreshoff designed the winning *Vigilant,* but two of the boats he defeated, the *Pilgrim* and the *Jubilee,* based on one of his creations, would be more significant in prefiguring today's competitive vessels. The challenge had become an opportunity to discover future sailboats worthy of becoming legends.

In 1895, Herreshoff faced the Earl of Dunraven's *Valkyrie III* with a radical boat, the *Defender,* its hull clad with bronze below the waterline and aluminum above. Corrosion due to electrolysis attacked the aluminum, and although it defeated the *Valkyrie,* the sailboat quickly became no longer seaworthy.

Eight years later, after winning in both 1899 and 1901 with the same boat, the *Columbia,* Herreshoff designed the *Reliance.* Words cannot describe this extraordinary vessel, its deep overhangs fore and aft making it nearly 130 feet long at the waterline, and carrying over 16,000 square feet of sail. A modern spirit and an avant-gardist, Nathanael Herreshoff transformed engineering into an art. The *Reliance* crushed the *Shamrock III.* For eighty years, this sloop remained the fastest monohull.

Celebrated clients of Louis Vuitton such as Cornelius Vanderbilt and J. Pierpont Morgan financed the victorious sailboats between 1893 and 1920. In effect, though officially the challenger was the owner, like Sir Thomas Lipton for example, the defense of the New York Yacht Club was subsidized by the largest fortunes in America, which, in the form of a syndicate, gave carte blanche to their architect.

SIR THOMAS LIPTON ENTRUSTED TO CHARLES E. NICHOLSON THE DESIGN OF HIS LATEST SAILBOAT: THE *SHAMROCK IV.*

Inexorably, the America's Cup continued to evolve. Sir Thomas Lipton entrusted to Charles E. Nicholson the design of his latest sailboat: the *Shamrock IV.* For the anticipated challenge of 1914, postponed until 1920 because of World War I, Nicholson designed a masterpiece that surprised everyone, not only with its design but also with its performance. With the weather in its favor, however, the defender, the slower *Resolute,* succeeded in saving face.

Between 1930 and 1937, J-class sailboats were at the forefront of progress, and the regattas took place in real time. In 1930, during the economic crisis, four candidates for the defense were put into the water. The triumphant *Enterprise,* co-owned and skippered by Harold S. Vanderbilt and nicknamed the "mechanical boat," was equipped with a riveted Duralumin mast. Four years later, the challenger *Endeavour* made use of the latest aeronautical technologies. It was a "perfect boat," according to Herreshoff himself. "Our Cup has never been in such great danger." But this advantage came to naught when the *Endeavour*'s crew struck, and were replaced by amateurs. On the water, the American sailors took advantage of every error to eke out the victory. The "Super J" *Ranger* of 1937 was methodically studied in the testing tank. Four models of that era, created by boat designers William Burgess and Olin Stephens, when tested with current analytical methods, proved themselves to be superior to the challenger *Endeavour II.*

The "Bollard," a bronze sculpture by visual artist Grégory Ryan, was given to the RYS by Yves Carcelle and Jean-Pierre Vivien, CEO and Vice-CEO of Louis Vuitton, on the occasion of the America's Cup Jubilee in 2001.
Photograph by Jon Nash/Archives Louis Vuitton

In 1958, the America's Cup returned to life with a new category of sailboat, the 12-meter, whose modest size suited the economic climate of the time. The constant search for perfection of architect Olin Stephens—a living legend who celebrated his hundredth birthday in 2008—resulted in seven America's Cup winners from 1958 to 1980.

In September 1967, the Frenchman Marcel Bich launched a challenge for 1970. The NYYC asked him to wait until 1973, since the Australians had already issued a challenge. But his determination was such, his insistence so persuasive, that he was finally given a chance to engage in a preliminary duel against the Australians. The NYYC modified their rules: henceforth, all challenges launched in the thirty days after the last regatta of the America's Cup would be accepted. Thus the way was paved for the Louis Vuitton Cup.

Sortie de Secours
110
LOUIS VU

From 1933 to 1938, Gaston-Louis, the son of Georges Vuitton, upon the initiative of his wife, developed a model boat division.
Thus, in 1935, one could acquire a scale model of the *North Star,* the steam-yacht owned by Cornelius Vanderbilt from 1902 to 1914, as well as one of the J-class *Endeavours*. These models were exhibited the following year at the International Nautical Trade Show in Paris.
Archives Louis Vuitton

UNE MALLE VUITTON ET VA-T'EN RASSURÉ.....
Confort et sécurité, telles sont les conditions essentielles d'un heureux voyage, éléments précieux que la marque VUITTON au prestige incontesté vous garantit de façon absolue ; pour bien voyager, ayez un trousseau de malles VUITTON dont les qualités de fabrication et de conception sont universellement réputées et composez vous-même ce trousseau par une sélection facile des innombrables modèles exposés au Vuitton Building ou par simple lettre à son bureau d'études qui vous adressera gracieusement tous plans et devis.
LOUIS VUITTON
PARIS 70 CHAMPS ELYSEES
NICE 12 AVENUE DE VERDUN
CANNES 10 RUE DES BELGES
LONDON 149 NEW BOND STREET

A publicity insert
in the June 1928 issue of *Vogue* says, "A Vuitton trunk and you're safely on your way..."
Archives Louis Vuitton

***Endeavour*, 1934:**
You can best appreciate the shape of the sails and truly feel the power of the boat tacking when it is running upwind. The English challenger had the bit between its teeth!
Photograph by Edwin Levick (The Mariners' Museum, Newport News, Virginia)

The interior of the *Galatea,* the challenger in 1886, was especially ornate, and the yacht was much admired by spectators upon its arrival in New York. After an extremely quick transatlantic crossing, Lieutenant William Henn, retired from the Royal Navy, and his wife arrived in New York to take part in the America's Cup. The wardroom of the *Galatea* had a surprising look for a racing sailboat, with its leopard-skin rugs, its draperies, its houseplants, and its objets d'art. Mrs. Henn even brought her monkey, Peggy. After the Cup, the couple crossed to the West Coast, where the *Galatea* spent the winter, returning the following year to Great Britain.

Photograph by Beken of Cowes

In 1930, the advanced technical capabilities of the American J-class boat the *Enterprise,* with its advanced Duraluminum mast, were subject to hot debate. The New York Yacht Club revised the regulations of the class, restricting the maneuvers allowed on boats' bridges. In particular, it required that sailboats be equipped in a manner that would allow the crew to live onboard.

On the 1934 defender, the *Rainbow,* the rules were implemented only at the most basic level, with tables and folding chairs such as the ones used for camping. To show their good faith, however, the crew of the *Rainbow* did actually live on the boat during the regattas.

Photograph by Edwin Levick (The Mariners' Museum)

Skipper Charlie Barr—photographed here behind boat owner Alexander Smith Cochran, gripping the helm. With his three consecutive wins in the America's Cup (1899, 1901, and 1903), Barr stood as an equal to Russell Coutts, who won in 1995, 2000, and 2003. His 1905 record for the fastest Atlantic Ocean crossing stood for seventy-five years, bested by Eric Tabarly only in 1980!

We have Barr to thank for the building of the legendary schooner *Westward*. In 1909, Barr told Alexander Smith Cochran about his superb 1904 season of sailing in the Solent and Kiel. Cochran then decided to have a schooner built for the regattas in Europe.

On March 31, 1910, the *Westward* was put into water in Bristol at Nathanael Herreshoff's shipyard. After a few attempts, the gigantic schooner (136 feet long and 96 feet at its waterline) departed for the old continent. In Europe, the *Westward* defeated all of its English and German competitors in the "Big Boat" J-class, even the kaiser's *Meteor IV*. On July 16, Charlie Barr wrote a letter to Herreshoff: "This boat is marvelous. We have met a few gusts, the water has never touched the bridge. Of eight races, we have won eight!" The *Westward* was to be the last boat captained by Charlie Barr; he died of a heart attack at the age of forty-seven, onboard off the coast of Southampton, on January 24, 1911.

Photograph by Edwin Levick (The Mariners' Museum)

Yachting and the America's Cup

have always been the passion of royalty and heads of state. Queen Victoria cruised on the schooner *America* on August 22, 1851, at the head of the fleet in the race around the Isle of Wight. One hundred and fifty years later, Princess Diana and Juan Carlos, the king of Spain, were at Cowes for the Jubilee. Kings of England Edward VII and George V contributed greatly to the training of the British challengers between 1893 and 1930.

President John F. Kennedy was always a sailor. His favorite boat, the *Royono,* a 1936 yawl almost 70 feet long, designed by John G. Alden, has been restored and still sails.

In his speech for the opening of the 1962 America's Cup on September 14 in Newport, President Kennedy said: "I really don't know why it is that all of us are so committed to the sea, except I think it is because, in addition to the fact that the sea changes and the light changes, and ships change, it is because we all came from the sea. And it is an interesting biological fact that all of us have in our veins the exact same percentage of salt in our blood that exists in the ocean, and therefore, we have salt in our blood, in our sweat, in our tears. We are tied to the ocean. And when we go back to the sea, whether it is to sail or to watch it, we are going back from whence we came."

Photograph by Robert L. Knudsen (John F. Kennedy Presidential Library and Museum, Boston, Massachusetts)

Built in Clyde in 1893 from a design by George L. Watson, at the same time as the royal sailboat *Britannia,* the *Valkyrie II* was slightly lower in the water than that boat, and proved to be faster. Here in the Solent, in a photograph by Beken, it shows impressive power.

On October 13, 1893, in New York, in the last round of the America's Cup, the wind was at 30 knots with violent gusts. The *Valkyrie II,* ahead at the buoy, seemed to be on her way to victory, setting her biggest balloon jib topsail. On the *Vigilant,* at battle stations, two men on the masts and another on the boom at water level responded, shaking out the reef in the mainsail and setting a balloon bowsprit spinnaker. Suddenly, the *Valkyrie*'s jib burst. Another was set quickly, only to share the same fate. Then the mainsail ripped, but a crew member was able to repair it in time. It was replaced by a large jib topsail, but it was too little, too late: *Vigilant* overtook *Valkyrie II,* and the finish line came up quickly. The defender had won the America's Cup for the third time.

Photograph by Beken of Cowes

NEWPORT 1983

For twenty-five years, from 1958 to 1983,
the Cup took place in Newport, Rhode Island. (Preceding spread) As the fog comes in at the end of the day, two boats are flying their spinnakers sail up to Castle Hill near the entrance of the Bay.
Photograph by Gilles Martin-Raget

It's rare for a photographer to be allowed to climb
to the masthead during the ballet that precedes a departure. (Above) Gilles Martin-Raget took this shot while the two 12-meter boats played cat and mouse.
Photograph by Gilles Martin-Raget

Chapter 2

The *Australia II* Wins the Louis Vuitton Cup and the America's Cup

Never before had there been so many 12-meters in Newport. Seven challengers to the New York Yacht Club were present the day after the 1980 America's Cup. Bruno Troublé, skipper of the French challenger, persuaded Louis Vuitton to become the official sponsor of the regattas that would decide which of the challengers would prevail. Five nations were represented: Australia (with three challengers), Canada, France, Great Britain, and Italy. The candidates would race two at a time to decide who would take on the American champion, the defender of the America's Cup. John Bertrand, on board the *Australia II,* equipped with an upside-down winged keel, dominated the selection process to win the Louis Vuitton Cup. After a memorable match against Dennis Conner's *Liberty,* he put an end to 132 years of American dominance and brought the America's Cup home to Perth, Australia.

The revolutionary keel of *Australia II* minimized its wetted surface area, making it easier to maneuver and, most importantly, lighter than the competition.
Photograph by Erwan Quéméré

For the 1983 race, the best challenger, having won the brand-new Louis Vuitton Cup, would be sent to meet the sailboat selected by the defense for the America's Cup in a single match. A trophy would also be given to the winner of each series of the preliminary regattas.

Since 1974, the Australian businessman Alan Bond had tried in vain to conquer the America's Cup. For this race, Bond gave his team the best foundation, using extensive research both in the field and with computer simulations. His architect, Ben Lexcen, inspired by recent developments in the 5.5-meter class, designed the most amazing 12-meter ever created, the *Australia II.* Stacking the deck in his favor, Bond then went into partnership with a Melbourne syndicate, which financed the construction of a more conventional sailboat, also designed by Lexcen, the *Challenge 12.*

From the very first matches, John Bertrand and the *Australia II* outclassed their adversaries. With her ability to make much tighter turns than her competitors, the *Australia II* had the advantage from the very start of every race. Since she was so light and carried more sail, her tacking acceleration was spectacular. She was also stiffer, listing less and catching the wind more effectively than any other boat. At each tack, she surprised everyone anew with her maneuverability. Finally, she rounded the buoy with the wind at her back.

Did she have a weakness? Possibly. As she was lighter than any 12-meter built in a long time, she also had the shortest waterline—speed is theoretically dependent on waterline length—in the history of the cup, though the slant of her elongated rear made up for this handicap. The effortless domination of the *Australia II* was certainly due to her keel, mysteriously hidden behind a green canvas "modesty skirt" and well-protected. No one had seen anything like it for a century—not since 1887, when the Scottish challenger the *Thistle* was put into the water at Clyde. While all of the other boats present belonged to the same design family as the preceding winners, the *Courageous* and the *Freedom,* Ben Lexcen had broken with tradition: the hull was only just above the waterline fore and aft, reducing the boat's wetted surface sharply. In addition, the inverted keel, with its thick fins, was very short, which explained her great maneuverability.

In the first round robin, where each boat was to meet her competitors twice, the *Australia II* was bested only once, by the *Challenge 12.* She trounced the British

THE EFFORTLESS DOMINATION OF THE *AUSTRALIA II* WAS CERTAINLY DUE TO HER KEEL, MYSTERIOUSLY HIDDEN BEHIND A GREEN CANVAS "MODESTY SKIRT" AND PROTECTED BY A VIGILANT ARMY.

Victory 83, for which Peter de Savary had enlisted no less than four of the highest-caliber skippers—Phil Crebbin, Harold Cudmore, Rodney Pattison, and Lawrie Smith—as well as about forty crew members and two architects, to put two *Victory*s in the water. But quantity is often the enemy of quality, and the English syndicate could not match the capacity of the Australian team. With the 1980 *France 3,* modified on a modest budget by architect Jacques Fauroux, the skipper Bruno Troublé had an uphill battle against the technical edge of the other challengers. Only the third Australian syndicate, directed by Syd Fischer, came close. Their *Advance,* designed with the help of an astonishing scale model by Alan Payne, lasted through twelve matches.

In Round Robin B, modeled after the first round robin, the placings remained the same, but the pressure created by the mysterious keel began to worry the defense. On July 24, Robert McCullough, ex-commodore of the NYYC and organizer of the event, sent a letter to American official Mark Vinbury questioning the legality of the *Australia II*'s keel. All the challenger candidates received copies of this letter, in an apparent attempt to sow strife and perhaps incite the challengers to protest against the Australians, but none took the bait. In fact, the boat had been measured on June 16 by three official measurers (who unanimously declared it legal); the NYYC, which had the right to send their own observer at this time, had missed the date!

The Americans also began to question the validity of the *Australia II*'s design on another front. According to the rules at the time, all team members had to be nationals of the country they represented. Back in 1980, the NYYC had allowed the Australians to use the Dutch testing tank at Wageningen. But now the Americans began to question whether Lexcen had in fact designed the craft, rather than one of the Dutch engineers, Peter Van Oossanen and Joop W. Sloff, who had worked with him in the Netherlands. While they searched for any possible way to disqualify the Australian craft, it was revealed that on July 24, the NYYC had secretly contacted the Dutch laboratory to draw up an identical keel for one of its own boats. As a last resort, some members of the club considered canceling the challenge.

While "Keelgate," as it was soon to be called, was getting a lot of ink, the *Australia II* continued its relentless series of victories, even if a few technical incidents darkened the picture. During a third match against *Canada I,* crew member John McAllister, climbing up the mast, had a bad fall, lost consciousness, and broke his arm. In the last round robin the rules were modified, reducing the number of regattas for the last two boats, the *France 3* and the *Advance.*

IN THE LAST RUNNING TACK, THE LIBERTY OUTDISTANCED THE *AUSTRALIA II.* THE PSYCHOLOGICAL PRESSURE WAS AT ITS HEIGHT.

The *Victory* carried itself honorably against the *Azzurra* and the *Canada I,* while the *Challenge 12* lost ground, apparently paying the price for a poorly adjusted new mast; it was eliminated at the end of these matches. In the semifinals and finals of the Louis Vuitton Cup, the *Victory* saved face by snatching one victory from the formidable Australians. Still, the *Australia II* won 48 of 54 matches over three months, and John Bertrand and Alan Bond received the Louis Vuitton Cup.

Dennis Conner obtained permission to run with three different measurement certificates, so that the configuration of his champion, the *Liberty,* could be adapted to suit the weather. In effect, while the challenger was required to define his sailboat precisely, the defense remained free to choose the configuration of his own.

After six of the seven America's Cup regattas, the *Liberty* and the *Australia II* stood at 3 to 3. The moment was historic: On Monday, September 26, 1983, the seventh match started. In the last running tack, the *Liberty* outdistanced the *Australia II.* The psychological pressure was at its height. Conner, already thinking of the last close-hauled tack, forgot to keep tabs on his pursuer. By the time he realized his error, it was too late, and he had been overtaken. The *Australia II* reached the buoy in the lead, and dodged into the last close-hauled tack for the victory. This American defeat, the first in 132 years, coincided with the birth of the Louis Vuitton Cup. A new era had begun.

Newport 1983:
The Australian *Challenge 12* chasing the British *Victory* during the first edition of the Louis Vuitton Cup. Very similar to the *Australia II* in terms of its waterline, but with a conventional keel, the *Challenge 12* served as its life-size test run.
Photograph by Guy Gurney

Even with three separate measurement certificates, the *Liberty* was unable to do much against the revolutionary keel of the *Australia II*. Before the last regatta, the seventh and ultimate, the defender returned to the shipyard at Cove Haven Marina to adapt the boat to the following day's forecast of low winds. Six days had gone by without Conner winning a single match. This would be his last one, anyway.

"Big Bad Dennis," shown here during the press conference after his defeat, had become merely mortal once again. He could not hold back his tears at his failure to retain the American domination of the America's Cup, even if his boat was clearly slower. Like a wounded hero in a western film, he vowed to personally avenge America's honor and recapture the precious trophy in Australia in 1987.

Photograph by Gilles Martin-Raget

Only the day before, John Bertrand had been polishing his pre-start technique, anxious to fine-tune his mastery of time and distance to the starting line before the battle was at its height.

Now, it was finished. The ordeal of the last months, when the defense was united in its attempt to disqualify his boat, was over. On that day, he only felt joy and astonishment. It was a triumphant John Bertrand, as shown above, who sat next to Dennis Conner, having snatched the Cup away after a hand-to-hand combat that would go down in history. Two hours earlier, he had been lagging far behind the American boat in the final regatta, and seemed to have no chance of winning. Even the press boat didn't think it possible, returning to port before the end of the race!

Photograph by Gilles Martin-Raget.

***France 3*, Baron Bich's last boat,**
reached the challengers' finals in 1980, the best French performance in the Louis Vuitton Cup. In 1983, despite modifications, this boat could not compete with an armada of newer designs. Skippered by Bruno Troublé, here it is seen head on, preparing to round the first buoy.
Photograph by Guy Gurney

AUSTRALIA II

Here is the terror of 1983, which put an end to 132 years of American domination over the Cup: the *Australia II*.

In his third attempt to take the Cup, Alan Bond understood that he couldn't beat the Americans with their own weapons. He set out instead to win by stealth: "Like robbing a bank," he said. It was he who encouraged innovative architect Ben Lexcen to try something else, and gave him the means to do it. A bit of a maverick, a humorist, and a little academic, Lexcen created a lighter, more maneuverable, and faster 12-meter that carried more sail, with the famous upside-down winged keel that changed the face of the America's Cup forever. It is no surprise that the defense protested against his invention: "We have always had the same problem here, since 1974, with every innovation; that is part of the nature of the America's Cup. They think that the keel is illegal because it is an element of speed and it can give us a chance to win."

Photograph by Christian Février.

FREMANTLE 1987

SAN DIEGO 1988

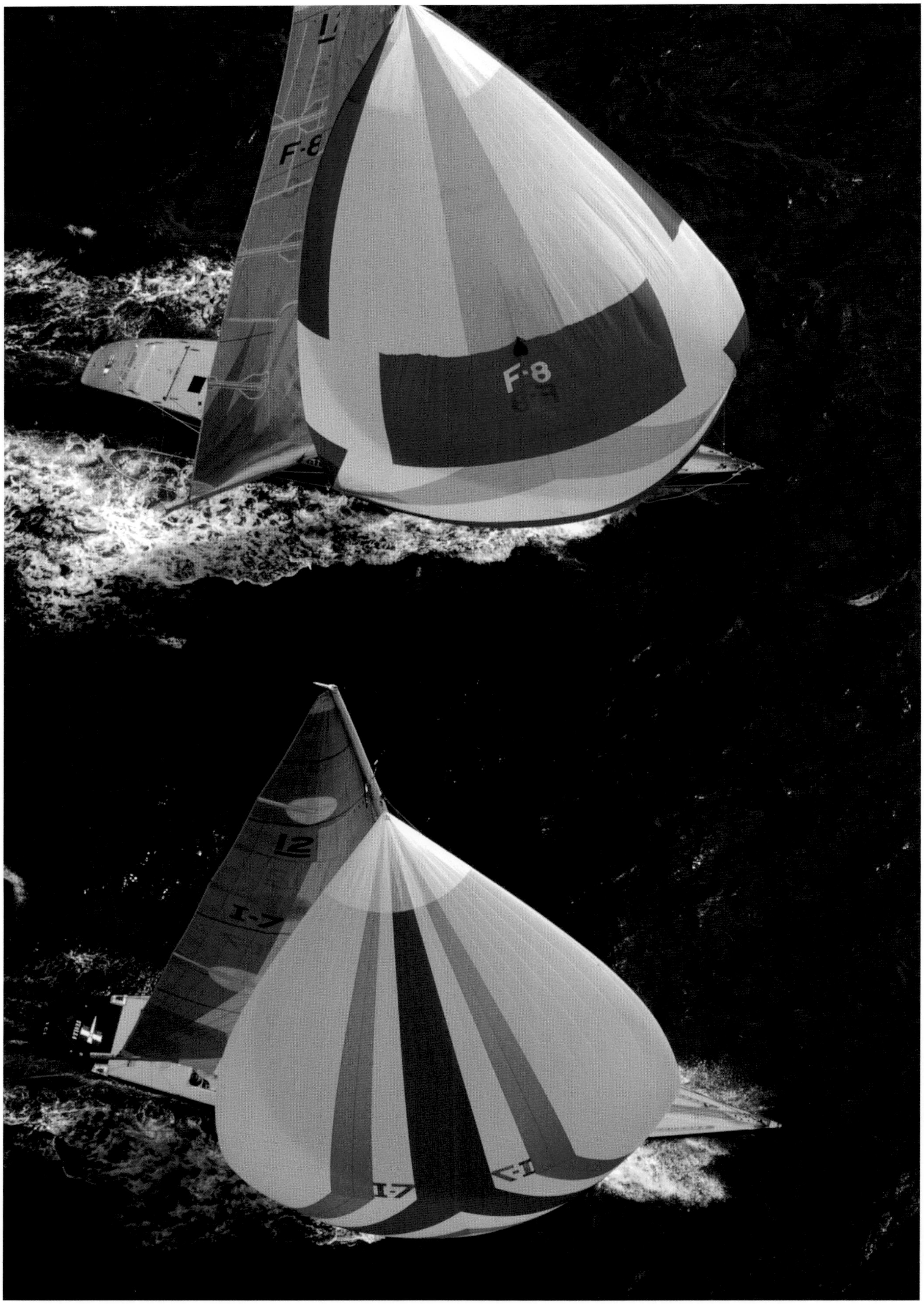

Just after the start of the Cup, the *Kookaburra III*
(preceding spread) managed to cross in front of the American challenger, Dennis Conner's *Stars & Stripes*. Yet it wouldn't repeat that exploit—the American would soon retake the lead and round all the buoys far ahead of its opponent. Payback for the humiliation of 1983!
Photograph by Philip Plisson/Pêcheur d'images

In the foreground, *Italia,*
commissioned by Maurizio Gucci, was a magnificent boat with such a dizzyingly attractive crew, that the restaurant Casa Italia became the most popular in Fremantle. (Above) Here she faces off against the *Challenge,* Yves Pajot's boat.
Photograph by Guy Gurney

Chapter 3

Dennis Conner's Revenge: The Americans in the Louis Vuitton Cup

The America's Cup, removed from its long-standing home, was now in Perth, on the west coast of Australia. The Americans would devote all their energy to retrieving it. Before they could do so, they would need to win another trophy: the Louis Vuitton Cup, the obligatory route to meet the defender. Dennis Conner and the New York Yacht Club were passionate about restoring their honor. In the first meetings, the young New Zealander skipper Chris Dickson, with his "Kiwi Magic," made their task difficult. After his victory over the defender, the *Kookaburra III,* in 1988, Conner matched the small catamaran *Stars & Stripes* against the huge monohull *New Zealand* in San Diego in an unusual challenge.

Though he didn't win, the impressively young Chris Dickson, at the helm of the "Plastic Fantastic"—the nickname given to the first America's Cup boat built of plastic—showed the entire world it would now have to reckon with New Zealand.
Photograph by Philip Plisson/Pêcheur d'images

The day after the *Australia II*'s victory in Newport in 1983, the United States was in shock. While before the oldest trophy in sports had been the coveted object of only a few privileged who tried in vain to vanquish the New York Yacht Club, the field could now become open for anyone to win back the America's Cup.

No less than twenty-four challenges were issued to the club defender, the Royal Perth Yacht Club. The Yacht Club Costa Smeralda, the first to issue its demands, was named the Challenger of Record, in charge of the terms and organization for the regattas that would determine the defender's opponent. Faced with this influx of candidates, the commodore of the club, Gianfranco Alberini, demanded an entrance fee to verify the financial resources of the candidates: The number of challengers thus sank from twenty-four to thirteen.

The size of the event necessitated a modification in the selections process. Louis Vuitton renewed its sponsorship. In Fremantle, it played the role of co-organizer, with a dozen maritime juries, creating a course committee, setting up general headquarters with a press center to accommodate two thousand journalists, and hiring about sixty staff.

The Americans were ready to do anything to recapture the America's Cup, and prepared for the event with undisguised mania. For some, it was a point of honor; for others, it seemed to approach a matter of life and death.

The New York Yacht Club's entry called itself the America II Syndicate, for the NYYC was set on avenging itself. Dennis Conner, heading the Sail America Foundation for the San Diego Yacht Club, was determined to salvage his reputation as a professional regattaist. The creator of the Newport Harbour Yacht Club's *Eagle Challenge* dreamed only of the club's rehabilitation after its defeat in 1983. The Golden Gate Challenge for the Saint Francis Yacht Club modestly named its 12-meter boats *USA I* and *USA II,* with architect Gary Mull announcing that *USA I* would be the most surprising. For his part, Leonard Greene, owner of the *Courageous IV*, modernized the victor of the 1974 and 1977 America's Cup.

Finally, the Chicago Yacht Club gave a nod to its location in the name of its challenge: the Heart of America Syndicate. This club, which is on the Great Lakes, had to ask for a dispensation, since all club challengers, after the donation of the Cup, must organize a yearly regatta on a water route open to the sea.

The *America II* boats embarking from Fremantle formed a veritable armada. The first of these three boats would be subjected to so many modifications that it was nicknamed "the Lego boat." Its skipper, the handsome Texan John Kolius, had the popular

THE NEWCOMER, THE NEW ZEALAND TEAM, HAD A VERY STRONG BEGINNING. WHILE ALL TWELVE OF ITS COMPETITORS HAD BOATS WITH ALUMINUM HULLS, THE THREE NEW ZEALAND VESSELS USED PLASTIC.

vote as the next victor. For his part, Dennis Conner was training in Hawaii, far from prying eyes, going out every day to test his four *Stars & Stripes* vessels in strong wind conditions similar to those he expected to meet in the final phases in Australia.

The Canadian team reappeared in the cup with the same sailboat they had used in 1983, sufficiently modified to be called the *Canada II.* The Italians returned with two challengers. The three *Azzurra*s of the Yacht Club Costa Smeralda were featured on the covers of all the yachting magazines, and the presence in the syndicate of names such as Gianni Agnelli, chairman of Fiat, and His Highness the Aga Khan, founder of the club, fueled dreams of victory. Consorzio Italia built two sailboats, the *Italia I* and the *Italia II,* the second of which sank the day of its launching. The challenge of the Royal Thames Yacht Club was directed by Harold Cudmore, whose reputation as an aggressive skipper was well established. His second sailboat, the *Crusader II,* nicknamed "the Hippo," easily surpassed the *USA I* in originality. For the French, a fratricidal conflict was taking place. The two Pajot brothers, Yves and Marc, silver medalists in the 1972 Olympics and world champions in 1976, were directing two challenges, Yves's *Challenge France,* which was operating on a tight budget, and Marc's *French Kiss,* whose name gave rise to several debates.

The newcomer, the New Zealand team, had a very strong beginning. While all twelve of its competitors had boats with aluminum hulls, the three New Zealand vessels used plastic. "Why build a plastic boat when all the others are built in aluminum, unless you're trying to cheat?" asked Dennis Conner during a Louis Vuitton press conference. In the first round robin, in October 1986, Chris Dickson, skipper of the *New Zealand KZ 7,* quickly rebaptized as the "Kiwi Magic" or the "Plastic Fantastic," hoisted himself up to be among the first three out of the water, with the *America II* and the *Stars & Stripes.* Harold Cudmore on the *White Crusader* and Tom Blackaller on the *USA II* found themselves tied for fourth place. The *Courageous* abandoned the course at the end of the matches, with a single victory against the *Challenge France.* In the following series, the "Kiwi Magic" arrived ahead of this regatta, John Kolius, beaten by Dennis Conner, arrived in second place; and Marc Pajot took a surprising third place before Blackaller, Conner, and Cudmore. The third round robin was determined with each victory counting twelve points. Dennis Conner was beaten by Blackaller, but still placed second behind Chris Dickson who earned another clear round; Pajot and Cudmore were selected for the semifinals, as they had been beaten by the other two.

DENNIS CONNER CRUSHED THE DEFENDER, 4 TO 0, DECLARING, "THIS IS NOT THE BEGINNING OF A DREAM, THIS IS THE END TO A NIGHTMARE."

Chris Dickson, who came to celebrate his twenty-five years, won 37 out of 38 matches. In the final of the Louis Vuitton Cup, up against a stirred-up Dennis Conner, well equipped against the strong wind that was predicted, Dickson took only a single regatta, the third. During a spectacular and close race, Conner made 55 successive tacks in 40 seconds. Practice and experience had spoken!

In the end, it took 219 selection matches to determine the two sailboats that would compete for the America's Cup, in which Dennis Conner crushed the Australian defender, 4 to 0, declaring, "This is not the beginning of a dream, this is the end to a nightmare." The American honor had been avenged!

However, the nightmare would return. During lunch at the San Diego Yacht Club on July 17, 1987, the New Zealand banker Michael Fay, taking literally the wording of the Deed of Gift, launched a rogue challenge asking the California club to respond to him on the water in ten months. The sailboat he proposed to use for this challenge was 90 feet (27 meters) long at the waterline—despite the mutual consensus that had reigned since 1958 that challengers and defenders of the America's Cup would compete in 12-meter boats. A judicial imbroglio began. Finally, Dennis Conner, forced by the courts to respond, took him on with a 60-foot (18-meter) high-tech catamaran fitted with a winged mast with articulated flaps, inspired by those seen on C-class boats.

The fantastic meeting between the hulking 90-foot monohull "Big Boat" and the ultrasophisticated 60-foot catamaran took place September 7–9, 1988. As expected, the multihull showed itself to be decisively faster, winning the 27th America's Cup.

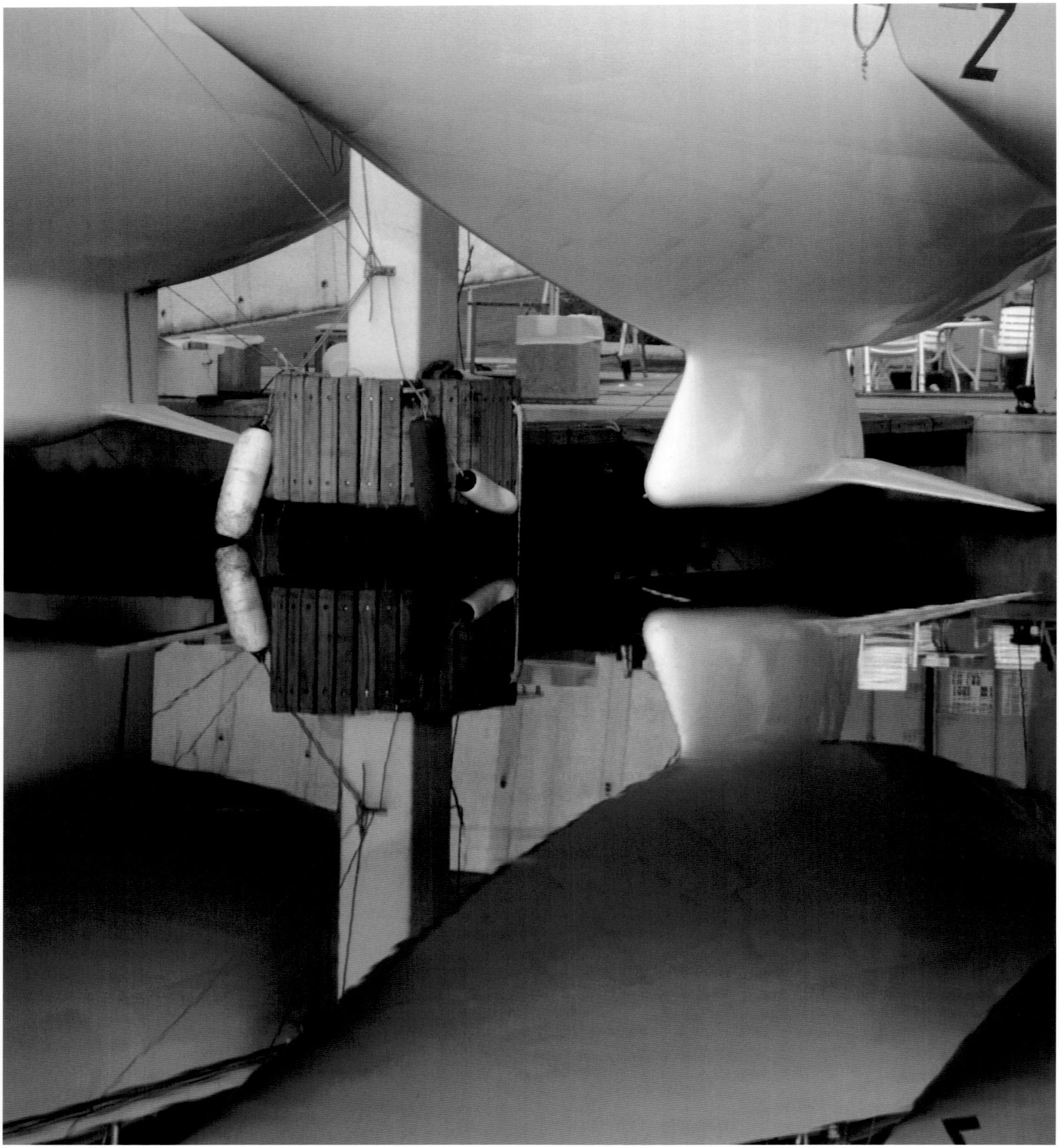

In 1987, four years after it was introduced,
the brilliant innovation of Australian architect Ben Lexcen attracted many emulators. It also influenced the design of keels on cruising sailboats.
Photograph by Gilles Martin-Raget

As is so often the case,
the *Stars & Stripes* had more trouble distancing itself from its New Zealand opponent in the finals of the Louis Vuitton Cup than in cruising to an easy victory in the America's Cup a few days later.
Photograph by Gilles Martin-Raget

FRENCH KISS

On these 20-meter sailboats, weighing more than twenty tons, it is not really necessary for the crew to counterbalance the boat, but psychologically it makes a difference. The *French Kiss,* designed by Philippe Briand, made good time in this Louis Vuitton Cup.

Marc Pajot met Tom Blackaller on the *USA* in the second round robin, and John Kolius on the *America II* in the third. It reached the semifinals, where it was eliminated 4 to 0 by the redoubtable Chris Dickson on the "Kiwi Magic."

Because of its elegance—and perhaps its racy name—the *French Kiss* earned tremendous press coverage. The very balanced lines of its hull made an impact on all who saw it, earning it considerable respect throughout the race.

Photograph by Philip Plisson/Pêcheur d'images

Before the start, Dennis Conner, onboard the *Stars & Stripes,* here takes a peek at his competitor from under the boom. Conner was at the top of his form here: Three-time winner of the America's Cup, he is also the guy who, in the name of America, lost it. In 1987, nothing would stop him—he was racing to win.

From the start, Conner knew that he must have a 12-meter that could outperform the rest, at least this one time, so he surrounded himself with the best. John Marshall managed a team of talented American architects—Britton Chance, Bruce Nelson, and David Pedrick—all strong personalities from a variety of backgrounds. He brought together scientists who had never seen a boat before but were able to precisely calculate the advantages of any design option. Every facet was reconsidered from the ground up, from the design of the hull to the analysis of theoretical performances, and approved by five sailors who stood at the top of their sport. This new approach left nothing to chance. In all areas—sails, strategy, communication—Conner surrounded himself with passionate, skilled specialists. Even the hull of his boat was covered in a material that resembled the skin of a dolphin, the fruit of research from the 3M Society's laboratories.

Photograph by Philip Plisson/Pêcheur d'images

As the saying goes, Conner "got the job done." After brooding over his defeat for four years, it was with relief that he renewed his status as an American legend. His victory would be proclaimed all over the American media, from *The New York Times* to *The Washington Post*. It was not easy, but Dennis Conner demonstrated that his professionalism was its own reward. Hundreds of hours spent at the helm, until he and his boat were truly one; systematic testing, over and over, of each sail setting, each condition of the sea, each maneuver, until it had become automatic: This was the price to pay for victory. Even the most gifted amateurs like Tom Blackaller, who loved to joke about the laborious side of Conner's method, were obliged to recognize its success. Conner prepared for the America's Cup in the same way that one would train for the Olympic Games, with a special dietary regime, physical workouts, medical surveillance, and absolute personal discipline. His two years of preparation were not in vain: he would bring the Cup home to his country.

Photograph by Philip Plisson/Pêcheur d'images

35
White Crusader

Harold Cudmore, the capricious Irish skipper, did his best to survive in the Louis Vuitton Cup. Here, he literally plows under a wave in pursuit of the *French Kiss,* tearing his jib. The *White Crusader* was the first boat in history to sometimes sail with a brand name—White Horse whiskey—on its spinnaker.
Photograph by Philip Plisson/Pêcheur d'images

The American challenger *Stars & Stripes*
overlooked forecasts of light wind in the first rounds of the Louis Vuitton Cup and becalmed in the weak wind, barely avoiding elimination. But in the final, with a strong wind blowing, it came back to life and did not give its opponents a chance. Here we see it dominating the challenger from New Zealand.
Photograph by Philip Plisson/Pêcheur d'images

Hoisted by his own petard:
Frustrated by American dawdling over the announcement of the next America's Cup, New Zealand banker Sir Michael Fay threw down a rogue challenge. Taking literally the wording of the original nineteenth-century document, the Deed of Gift, he announced the construction of a single-hull yacht over 130 feet long. The San Diego Yacht Club accepted the challenge with a 60-foot catamaran. Whether it was really necessary to organize an America's Cup to prove that a catamaran is faster than a single-hull yacht remains a good question.
Photograph by Guy Gurney

A picture worth a thousand words:
The *Stars & Stripes,* the American dragonfly,
toys with the ponderous New Zealand whale.
Photograph by Christian Février

SAN DIEGO 1992

Climbing to the masthead
on America's Cup Class boats was not unusual and (preceding spread) crew members were used to being at 106 feet above deck.
Photograph by Guy Gurney

Losing 3 to 1 in the finals of the Louis Vuitton Cup,
(above) the Italian boat *Il Moro di Venezia V* launched a psychological attack on the New Zealand team by protesting its use of the bowsprit during spinnaker maneuvers.
Photograph by Carlo Borlenghi/Sea & See/DPPI

Chapter 4

New Class, Newcomers: Italy Has the Wind in its Sails

For the first time in the history of the Cup, in 1992, a new class was created: the International America's Cup Class (IACC), built to a design rule, larger, with more sail, and more modern than the 12-meter.

Thirteen nations took part in the venture. Newcomers Russia, England, Scotland, Denmark, Switzerland, and Croatia were forced to pull up, but Japan and Spain were among the seven teams to finish the race. About twenty sailboats were constructed to participate in the Louis Vuitton Cup in San Diego, California. The Italian Raul Gardini declared his intentions to construct five versions of *Il Moro di Venezia.* He came away with the Louis Vuitton Cup, but acknowledged the formidable organization of defender Bill Koch and his *America³.*

In 1992, Bill Koch, king of technology and art collector, victoriously defended the America's Cup. In 1995, he launched a new challenge, which would use an all-woman crew.
Photograph by Christian Février

The day after Dennis Conner's victory in 1987, the San Diego Yacht Club received twenty-two challenges. Since the America's Cup was no longer exclusively American, the silver cup seemed more accessible than ever, and thus attracted a number of contenders. Although Michael Fay's rogue challenge had not succeeded in taking the America's Cup away from California, the 1988 mismatch did open the way to the development of the new America's Cup Class of boat, more suited than the 12-meters to the notoriously fickle and light winds off Point Loma.

While the catamaran *Stars & Stripes* was crushing the "Big Boat" on the water, on land the discussions were already well under way. In the Louis Vuitton America's Cup Media Center, an old prison completely transformed by Vuitton to welcome the entire world press and all of the cup players, the first meetings took place to define a new type of sailboat. Twenty-two architects were soon concentrating on elaborating the IACC formula. The result was a sailboat inspired by the Maxi boat, a large, resolutely modern racing yacht. Compared to the 12-meter, the America's Cup Class was longer by four meters, bigger, had much more sail area, and was relatively lighter. Eighty percent of its weight was situated in the ballast four meters under the water, and it was constructed with modern materials: carbon fiber sandwiching, a core of honeycomb weave for the hulls, and titanium for the blocks and such.

The cup became a global event. Many of the challengers—two Russian teams, and one each from Croatia, Denmark, Switzerland, England, and Scotland—did not make it in the end, but one can still see the aluminum IACC built in Russia in a San Diego museum, and a mahogany hull made by a Croatian-Slovene group in former Yugoslavia found refuge in Venice after the first Serbo-Croatian conflicts.

In the end, seven nations and eight challengers—some with the financial means to build several boats—participated in the third Louis Vuitton Cup beginning on January 25, 1992: the *Il Moro di Venezia* (five IACC boats), the *New Zealand* (four boats), the *Nippon* (three boats), the *Ville de Paris* (three boats), the *España* (two boats), the *Spirit of Australia,* the *Challenge Australia,* and the Swedish *Tre Konor.*

Many things had changed since the last cup. The course now included three long legs called the "Z," where the sailboats raced quickly. Also, in order to increase media exposure over the competition—ESPN had acquired the television rights—the names of sponsors could be placed on the ship's hulls and spinnakers. Louis Vuitton strengthened its role as co-organizer of the Louis Vuitton Cup, on both land and water, and on-the-water umpires, at Tom Ehman's suggestion, now followed the boats, settling disagreements on the spot, and penalizing faults with penalty turns, a turn through at least 270 degrees of arc, which must be completed before the finish line. This marked the end of the era when skippers spent long evenings defending themselves before the international jury.

PAUL CAYARD CALLED OUT TO HIS COLLEAGUES, "THE KIWIS ARE NAVIGATING WITH A FORK!"

The Louis Vuitton Cup played out as a dizzying series of flip-flops between the different syndicates. The pattern was set early: In the first round robin the Japanese beat the Italians—who went off course; in the next round robin New Zealand was brushed aside by the Italians; and in turn they were defeated by the French. Paul Cayard, skipper of *Il Moro di Venezia V,* accused Rod Davis on the *New Zealand* of deliberately slowing down. Iain Murray, skipper of the *Spirit of Australia,* in third with three points, chose to abandon the last two rounds of the race to profoundly remodel his boat.

Since the 1983 controversy over the unusual keel of *Australia II,* competing yachts' keels had been, for the most part, kept discreetly hidden under tarpaulins. But in the clear California waters, it was sometimes possible to see the shape of a yacht's keel under water. During the press conference after the second day of the regattas, Paul Cayard called out to his colleagues, "The Kiwis are navigating with a fork!" A journalist responded, "And what about you?" He answered, "No, we're normal, we have a spoon." The architect of the *New Zealand,* Bruce Farr, had given the boat a tandem keel, with two fins that could move independently, taking on the function of rudder. Iain Murray (*Spirit of Australia*) also had an "exotic" keel under his hull, but it did not seem very well designed. The *Nippon,* with Chris Dickson at the helm, had a "duck" design, similar to the *USA II* of 1987, with twin rudders, one just aft of the bow.

Soon four challengers had left the scene. At this stage of the competition, to pay homage to the elegant and efficient way of those (still present) who made the event possible, Bruno Troublé, Jean-Marc Loubier, and the Louis Vuitton crew, organized a wonderful Thousand and One Nights party on the aircraft carrier *USS Kitty Hawk.*

During the third and last round robin, Chris Dickson (*Nippon*) was in top form: His boat made the best of the mounting wind, especially in the close-hauled tacks, and won all the legs of the series. The *New Zealand* came in second. Paul Cayard and Marc Pajot saved their bacon and were selected for the semifinals. Iain Murray was upset; it would be the first time since 1967 that Australia would be absent from the America's Cup. In the semifinals, a few incidents clouded the issue: the *Nippon* broke its rudder blade, the *Ville de Paris* ran into the *Nippon,* the *New Zealand* touched a buoy, then the *Nippon* broke its boom at the start, resulting in an annulled match. Finally, in nine courses, Chris Dickson and Marc Pajot had only managed three victories, and were thus eliminated.

AT EVERY PRESS CONFERENCE, RAUL GARDINI AND PAUL CAYARD COMPLETELY DESTABILIZED THE KIWIS.

The final of the Louis Vuitton Cup was a dramatic affair. The two protagonists were the products of very different architects. German Frers, creator of the five *Il Moro di Venezia* vessels, concentrated on the effectiveness of a powerful hull, while the New Zealander Bruce Farr relied on speed, preferring a lighter sail with less cloth. The debate took place not only on the water, but also very much on land: at every press conference, tensions rose. Raul Gardini, a brilliant businessman, and Paul Cayard, with no lack of humor, completely destabilized the Kiwis, who were leading 4 to 1. Only one more defeat away from elimination, Cayard protested against New Zealand's use of the bowsprit during spinnaker maneuvers; he won the protest, and the race was annulled, putting the score back to 3 to 1. The Italians won the next race, and the *Il Moro di Venezia V* again filed a complaint about the way Rod Davis's crew was attaching the spinnaker to the spinnaker pole, by using a rope attached to the bowsprit. This allowed the New Zealanders to use a lighter spinnaker pole and to build a lighter bow, making it easier to move the massive sails from one side of the boat to the other on a jibe. Though IACC rules did not forbid this use in the Louis Vuitton Cup, the defenders did not agree. New Zealand abandoned its controversial use of the bowsprit, and Michael Fay replaced Rod Davis with Russell Coutts, who had only helmed the tandem-keeled *New Zealand NZL 20* three times previously. Cayard took advantage of this change to win the two last matches and claim the Louis Vuitton Cup.

In the America's Cup, Paul Cayard beat Buddy Melges on the *America*^{3} by three seconds in the second course, but he could not do more. The *America*^{3} took the wind better, and was just barely fast enough to keep the cup in San Diego.

With private charter planes from all over the world, 6,000 extras, and 450 gondolas, the christening ceremony for the first *Il Moro di Venezia* in Venice, orchestrated by Franco Zeffirelli, was one of the biggest parties ever organized before the Salute. During a private black-tie dinner for forty guests in his fourteenth-century palace, Raul Gardini set the tone: "You are here at my home. This house was built forty years before Christopher Columbus discovered America. You could say that the America's Cup really doesn't impress me!"

Photograph by Carlo Borlenghi/Sea & See/DPPI

In 1992, a new boat was introduced to the America's Cup: the America's Cup Class. Longer, lighter, and with more sail than the 12-meters, these boats were also better adapted to the mild weather expected in southern California. This running tack shows as much: here, *Ville de Paris* and *Il Moro di Venezia V.*
Photograph by Guy Gurney

QANTAS
GM
HOLDEN

This new scale of America's Cup Class
gave boat designers the illusory feeling that the global hierarchy could be challenged. Infatuated with the famous winged keel of 1983, many architects strayed off the beaten path to experiment with revolutionary ideas. The "tandem" keel of the *Spirit of Australia* turned out not to be such a good idea, and the boat was soon eliminated from the Louis Vuitton Cup.
Photograph by Carlo Borlenghi/Sea & See/DPPI

The Japanese stepped into the ring for the first time in 1992,
bringing Asia into the America's Cup, the symbol of Western capitalism. Skippered by Chris Dickson, *Nippon,* the boat of the rising sun, was no embarrassment, but proved too slow to take center stage.
Photograph by Guy Gurney

Designed by Philippe Briand, *Ville de Paris*
was a good boat that performed well in any conditions. It would take the originality of the New Zealand sailboat and all of American skipper Paul Cayard's skill on *Il Moro di Venezia V* to keep it out of the challengers' finals.
Photograph by Philip Plisson/Pêcheur d'images

The *New Zealand* architect Bruce Farr found a radical solution to reduce his boat's weight at the front: the bow was truncated. Instead, to move the spinnaker pole, he added a boom (the white projection in the photo). While nothing prevents it from holding the spinnaker pole—on which the crew member is sitting—race rules do not allow it to be used to hold or pull in the spinnaker directly, without the spinnaker pole. This is precisely the point on which Cayard and Gardini issued their complaint, accusing the Kiwis of cheating and creating considerable ill will between the competitors. Losing 1 to 4, they were thus able to annul one of the regattas and to come back and win the Louis Vuitton Cup, 5 to 3.

Photograph by Guy Gurney

In the days before carbon mainsail battens,
the epoxy resin ones used to break easily: Here a crew member of the *Il Moro di Venezia V* climbing to the masthead to assess the damage.
Photograph by Philip Plisson/Pêcheur d'images

There was good cause for Italian jubilation
when Yves Carcelle awarded their team the Louis Vuitton Cup: *Il Moro di Venezia V* seemed touched by the hand of God having rallied from being under 1 to 3 to winning 5 to 3—what a relief! After such an impressive win, the crew was convinced that it would leave the defender standing. A few days later, they had to change their tune when faced with the technological advances made by the American team of architects and engineers coordinated by Bill Koch.
Photograph by Gilles Martin-Raget

43

SAN DIEGO 1995

The Kiwis
(preceding spread) and the pelican—quite a mascot.
Photograph by Christian Février

Shadow play under the California sun:
(Above) Sometimes the wind did not pick up until the late afternoon.
Photograph by Gilles Martin-Raget

Chapter 5

Black Magic Dominates: The America's Cup Leaves for New Zealand

This cup was decidedly different, bringing new surprises for both challengers and defenders each day. The Louis Vuitton Cup was particularly lively in San Diego: the 20-ton ballast bulb and keel of the *France 2* broke free and sank, capsizing the boat, which was recovered. Under the eye of the onboard television cameras, the *oneAustralia* broke in two in the middle of the regatta, a first in the history of the cup, and sank within two minutes. On Team New Zealand's *Black Magic,* Russell Coutts was practically unbeatable during the challenger selection, passing all of the buoys of the America's Cup ahead of Dennis Conner, this time at the helm of the *Young America* and not the *Stars & Stripes.*

Totally invested in the New Zealand challenge, Peter Blake managed to rally his country with a campaign inspired by his lucky red socks; New Zealanders bought red socks by the thousands, filling the team's coffers.
Photograph by Gilles Martin-Raget

Rumor had it that each crew member of Team New Zealand came on board with his own snacks, as the budget didn't allow for feeding the members of the challenge. It was also revealed that the *Black Magic NZL 32* had been beaten by the old *New Zealand NZL 20* during the trials in Auckland. Architect Bruce Farr, creator of the *NZL 20* and of Chris Dickson's last boat, the *NZL 39,* affirmed that he had never seen the boat in the water, which itself suggested that it wasn't very good. In fact, both the *NZL 32* and *Black Magic II NZL 38* sailed out of San Diego Bay early in the morning, not to return until late in the evening, as they prepared for the race. Peter Blake remained silent, kept a low profile, and answered all questions concerning their activities with a laconic "We are very busy." He also declined an invitation to the world championship to be held October 28–November 5, 1994.

The big news was revealed by Bill Koch before this championship: his defense candidate the *Mighty Mary* was all set—with an all-woman crew! John Bertrand's syndicate and his new *oneAustralia AUS 31,* with Rod Davis at the helm, dominated the competition early on, followed by the *Nippon* with John Cutler at the helm. The regattas floating in the San Diego Bay introduced these great sailboats to a populace who were amused to see women, during one race, arriving in the lead, a boat flying the colors of Russia chasing them in California.

Months before the first regattas of the Louis Vuitton Cup, the seven challengers were already in place in San Diego. The *France 2* underwent repairs to the lifting winch on its bridge, while the Japanese, working secretly behind palisades, remodeled their

Nippon JPN 30—which had proved disappointing in the first tests—so much that the other challengers submitted a complaint.

To reduce costs—the 1992 Cup had cost a fortune, about $350 million—the San Diego Yacht Club had decided to limit the number of sailboats built by challengers to two and the number of sails to forty-five. Another change was made to make the event more media-friendly: the sailboats would be unveiled to the public before the semifinals of the Louis Vuitton Cup and the Citizen Cup, the defense's selection series.

On the first day of the Louis Vuitton Cup, January 17, in a major upset, the *Nippon* beat the *oneAustralia,* Marc Pajot's *France 2*—nicknamed "the aircraft carrier" because of its enormous size—and the *Sydney 95*—Syd Fischer's fourth Louis Vuitton Cup boat. Russell Coutts, on his *Black Magic II NZL 38,* trounced the *Rioja de España,* coming in with more than ten minutes to spare. The next day, Syd Fischer, besting the *Rioja de España,* racked up two victories, doubling his 1992 final results. The following day, aboard Chris Dickson's *NZL 39,* crew member Steve Cotton lost the tips of two fingers

ANOTHER CHANGE: THE SAILBOATS WOULD BE UNVEILED TO THE PUBLIC BEFORE THE SEMIFINALS OF THE LOUIS VUITTON CUP AND THE CITIZEN CUP.

in a pulley. The *Nippon* won enough points to stay in the race. On the other hand, the two Kiwi boats beat the *oneAustralia,* which took third place in the round robin, *Black Magic* finishing in first place.

In the Louis Vuitton press rooms in San Diego, Paris (in the Louvre), Sydney, and Tokyo, the video Numéris sent did not reveal much through the California fog. But thanks to the virtual reality system arranged by Louis Vuitton—the first time in the world of sports that this system had been used—nothing escaped the viewer. These computer-generated images, provided by Medialab, an affiliate of Canal Plus, showed the boats that had run aground, gone off course, wrecked, or blown a spinnaker. If they were lacking in detail, they still supplied a mass of information on the contest as it progressed.

In the second round robin, the *oneAustralia* lodged a protest against Team New Zealand. Murray Jones, the New Zealand tactician, spent his time atop the mast, observing the wind zones and molding the mainsail by tapping its battens from above. When the sailboat listed, Jones was out over the water beyond the deck. Because of this the jury decided in favor of Australia, giving them the victory.

On February 4, fog had covered the three racing areas when the aircraft carrier *Abraham Lincoln* crossed into the ongoing match between the *Black Magic* and the *France 3.* The IACC boats were made totally of carbon, and the patrol boats, which for the most part were completely at a standstill, hardly registered on the radar. The captain became worried only when he saw a yellow Louis Vuitton buoy!

On February 20, the *France 2* had returned to training; as it sailed over the bar at the entrance to Mission Bay, skipper Peponnet called Marc Pajot on his mobile phone, announcing, "I have bad news, Marc: the keel is gone!" Having lost his training ship, Marc resigned himself to the fact that he was dogged by misfortune.

After all of these incidents, the most incredible thing happened. In full regatta against the *Black Magic,* the *oneAustralia AUS 35* broke in two, sinking within two minutes. The crew was rescued, and Peter Blake abandoned the race to come to their aid. The Australians had lost their best sailboat, but they took it in stride and immediately prepared the *AUS 31,* having lost a day of racing, to the benefit of Marc Pajot, who unfortunately would not have a better chance later.

The *Nippon*, whose skipper, Makoto Namba, was unanimously liked, could not hold off the attacks of the three other semifinalists, and won none of the eleven matches. Team New Zealand had brought out its second boat, the *Black Magic NZL 32,* about which nothing was known, even if rumors were flying. In fact, Russell Coutts was already passing all of the buoys in the lead and, once selected, preferred to train with the *NZL 38,* giving the points to his competitors. In the Louis Vuitton Cup finals, the *oneAustralia* avenged its honor by arriving fifteen seconds in front of the *Black Magic* in the fourth regatta—the New Zealand boat's only defeat on the water—although it was beaten 5 to 1.

IN FULL REGATTA AGAINST THE *BLACK MAGIC*, THE *ONEAUSTRALIA AUS 35* BROKE IN TWO, SINKING WITHIN TWO MINUTES.

The Citizen Cup ran simultaneously with the Louis Vuitton Cup, in four round robins between Bill Koch's female crew on the *Mighty Mary,* Dennis Conner's *Stars & Stripes,* with Paul Cayard at the helm, and the *Young America,* helmed by Kevin Mahaney and with a hull decorated by Pop artist Roy Lichtenstein. Dennis Conner won the final series of regattas by one point, but he had always dominated before, so he chose to enter the America's Cup sailing the *Young America.* In the cup, the challenger must specify his sailboat beforehand, while the defender can wait until the very day the matches begin. It was no use, though; the 29th America's Cup was a total defeat for the defense. The *NZL 32* took more wind, was faster, and was helmed by the three-times world champion of the match race. The *Black Magic* led at all thirty marks over the five contests to an uncontested America's Cup win in Auckland.

Did Team New Zealand have a secret? The answer was given by Doug Peterson, co-architect with Laurie Davidson, who said, "We have involved every member of the crew in designing the *Black Magic.*" Dennis Conner concluded, "Long live the America's Cup in New Zealand."

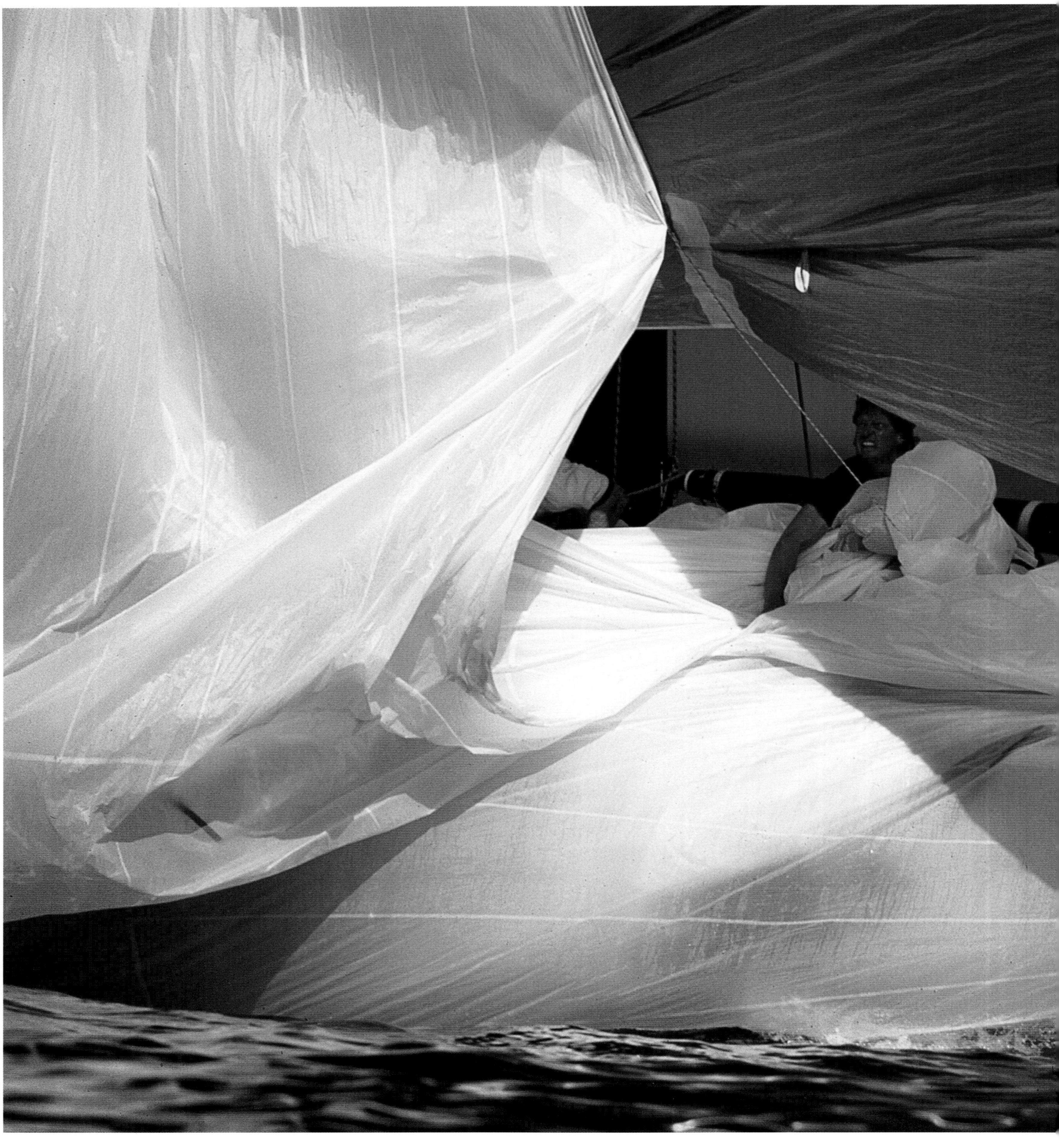

Twelve years after his historical victory in 1983,
Australian national hero John Bertrand returned to the America's Cup, the only real threat to Peter Blake and Russell Coutts' New Zealand boat, the *Black Magic*. Though the dramatic demise of his number-one boat was certainly a setback, Bertrand probably wouldn't have been able to defeat the Kiwis anyhow.
Photograph by Guillaume Plisson/Pêcheur d'images

A quintessential image of the match race—
the regatta duel. In the distance, a "pair" of boats face off, their spinnakers ballooning, while in the foreground the leader of another match sets off.
Photograph by Christian Février

Fog played tricks on the organizers of the Louis Vuitton Cup.
One day, an aircraft carrier crossed into the race area, and the regatta had to be cancelled. The photographers, however, were delighted.
Photograph by Carlo Borlenghi/Sea & See/DPPI

One of the highlights of the entire history of the Louis Vuitton Cup, and without a doubt of the America's Cup: On March 5, 1995, the *oneAustralia,* in a race against the New Zealanders on a strong sea and in the fog, literally broke in two just behind the mast, during the second upwind leg of the course. Rod Davis, the helmsman, asked Iain Murray, who not only handled the mainsail but was one of the boat's designers, "Big fella, are we sinking? . . . My God, we are sinking!" The crew jumped ship and was quickly rescued by nearby support boats, and Peter Blake and *Black Magic II* abandoned the race to lend a hand. In two minutes the boat sank to the bottom of the ocean. In the rain and the fog, no photographers were there, nor were there helicopters to transmit the images. Luckily George Johns, one of the many cameramen for the Louis Vuitton Cup, was not far away. He had the presence of mind to shoot the whole scene without interruption—an image for eternity.

Photograph by Gilles Martin-Raget

TAG
TAG

Chris Dickson returned to the race thanks to Tag Heuer.
Yet his budget was very limited and journalists were forced to refer to the *NZL 39*, the boat without a name, as the "Tag Heuer." Designed by the high-profile architect Bruce Farr, it performed well but bowed before the power of Peter Blake.
Photograph by Guillaume Plisson/Pêcheur d'images

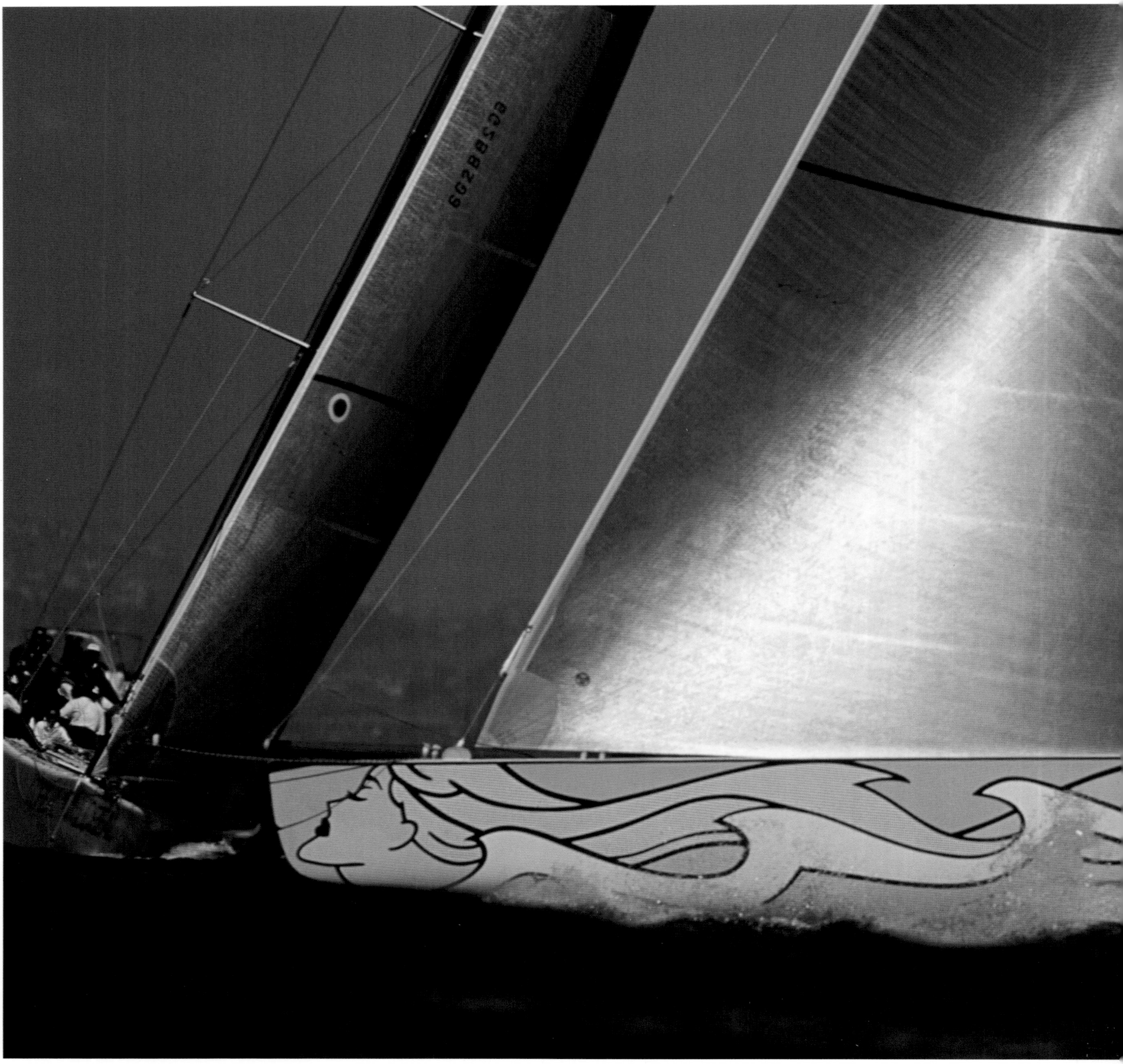

The best America's Cup Class boat for the defense, the *Young America,* was decorated by the pop artist Roy Lichtenstein, making Bruce Nelson's boat into an artistic masterpiece. The *Young America* was finally selected to race in the finals—an honor, certainly, but one that came with some pain! The situation at the end of the Citizen Cup, the selection process for the defender of the America's Cup, was ambiguous. The women on board the *Mighty Mary* had put up a good fight against both the *Young America* and the *Stars & Stripes*. In the semifinals, they had a better score than Dennis Conner, but the *Young America* was still given the lead. In the final, run in thirteen matches, Conner came in first, but won by only one point over the *Young America,* and by two points over the *Mighty Mary.* On the other hand, he won the right to choose his boat and his crew, a privilege of the defense (the challenger must declare his boat before the final of the Louis Vuitton Cup), and chose to sail the *Young America* rather than the *Stars & Stripes* in the America's Cup. Whether it was skippered by Dennis Conner or Paul Cayard, however, *Young America* was almost absurdly outclassed by Peter Blake's much faster *Black Magic,* helmed by Russell Coutts.

Photograph by Gilles Martin-Raget

AUCKLAND 2000

The spinnaker skimming over the surface of the water—
(preceding spread) though not intentional, it makes the photographer's day.
Photograph by Christian Février

Nature is far more powerful in Auckland,
than in San Diego. (Above) The wind being far stronger, it gave rise to the kind of face-off you rarely see in lighter weather.
Photograph by Carlo Borlenghi/Sea & See/DPPI

Chapter 6

The *Luna Rossa* Runs Aground Before the *Team New Zealand*

With sixteen challengers registered (including China, Russia, and Great Britain, who were not able to compete), eleven challengers from seven nations lined up at the Viaduct Basin in Auckland, New Zealand. Australia was present again, with the smallest budget and the youngest crew in history.

This time again, the Italians were first on the scene. Francesco de Angelis, at the helm of the *Luna Rossa,* established himself against five American challengers. In the beautiful final of the Louis Vuitton Cup, the *Luna Rossa* snatched victory from the *AmericaOne,* helmed by Paul Cayard, in a series of regattas for the history books. But he could do nothing against the formidable Russell Coutts, and the America's Cup stayed in New Zealand.

After the crushing victory of the *Black Magic* in 1995, Russell Coutts was the most formidable player in the 2000 America's Cup. No challenger had a chance; he easily won the Cup a second time.
Photograph by Francois Mousis

For the first time in the history of the America's Cup, there was no selection among the defenders; the *Team New Zealand* stood alone before the challengers. Thus, one might think that the Louis Vuitton Cup would be decisive. However, from the start of the 194 regattas of the Louis Vuitton Cup on October 18, 1999, the memory of Team New Zealand's victory in San Diego hung like a dark shadow over the waters of Hauraki Bay. In fact, two dark sailboats could be seen cruising past each other every morning, not far from the area set aside for the Louis Vuitton Cup matches. After Team New Zealand's practically unchallenged domination of the 1995 America's Cup, the team's sponsors renewed their contracts the day after the victory.

On the flat waters off Auckland, wind and water conditions were totally different from those in San Diego: not much swell, but a choppy sea that could make the sailboats plunge and drag, and a wildly variable wind. Sometimes in the middle of the course one could see, as if in a photomontage, two boats whose spinnakers were blowing in opposite directions. The volcanic islands that border the bay caused violent air currents that defied attempts to calculate weather conditions.

The round robin course was only 12.5 nautical miles long, with only two round trips, between the departure and the windward marker, though the following races would be run over three circuits. The first two days, the matches followed at a rate of ten each day, each of the rivals meeting with two adversaries. Quickly, three dominant syndicates emerged.

The Italian challenger, Prada Challenge, exuded elegance, discretion, team spirit, and efficiency from the beginning. The industrialist Patrizio Bertelli knew how to surround himself with worthy men, and provided them with ample means to reach their highest ambitions. He clearly declared his intention: "People think that we are participating in the America's Cup to promote our brand, but that is not the case. We are here to win." For the design of their two *Luna Rossa* sailboats, Bertelli chose Doug Peterson, who had worked on the last two winners of the America's Cup, and German Frers, the creator of *Il Moro di Venezia,* winner of the 1992 Louis Vuitton Cup. Rod Davis, now on his eighth Cup, led the navigation team, while logistics were entrusted to Laurent Esquier, with experience since 1974. His choice of skipper surprised the experts, but the Neapolitan Francesco de Angelis made an imposing figure in the competition, his personality perfectly matching the image of his sailboat. Towering above his crewmen, he set out at the start of each match with a lofty serenity, always at full speed, the perfect picture of a skipper in harmony with his boat. A little inexperienced

THE BRAZILIAN TORBEN GRAEL, TRIPLE OLYMPIC MEDALIST, HAD A SIXTH SENSE FOR TELLING WHICH WAY THE WIND WOULD BLOW.

in match races, he nevertheless quickly raised himself to the level of the best. *Luna Rossa* finished the series in the lead, without the slightest error.

If asked which tack he started on at the beginning of the race, on the starting line, de Angelis would respond, "Ask my tactician, I just do what he tells me to." This talented tactician, the Brazilian Torben Grael, triple Olympic medalist, had a sixth sense for telling which way the wind would blow. Torben's performance, assisted by a weather crew combing the surface of the water for clues throughout the Louis Vuitton Cup, was nothing short of inspired.

The New York Yacht Club once again asked John Marshall, president of North Sails, from which he organized Dennis Conner's 1987 recapture of the America's Cup, to direct its challenge, dubbed *Young America.* Marshall retained as architects Bruce Farr and Duncan MacLane, one of the creators of the winged mast of the *Stars & Stripes* catamaran in 1988, as well as enlisting Dr. Jerry Milgram, director of the technical team of *America^3,* winner of the 1992 America's Cup. As skipper, Marshall chose Ed Baird, who had guided the second *Team New Zealand* sailboat in the last challenge. Who better than he could know Russell Coutts, the man who manned the defenders' helm and terrorized everyone in Auckland? But before meeting the Kiwis, he would first need to win the Louis Vuitton Cup—and no one is immune from mishap, be it a spinnaker falling in the water or some graver incident.

For his part, Paul Cayard, America's Cup skipper since 1992, had a claim to be the most seasoned on America's Cup Class boats after Russell Coutts, though he hadn't won the 1992 Louis Vuitton Cup. Paul mounted a proper challenge aboard *AmericaOne.* Despite a few problems—among them the withdrawal of James H. Clark, president of Netscape Communications, as his principal sponsor, forcing him to search again for funding—he was able to bring together a solid and very competitive crew.

Louis Vuitton, with two New Zealand computer companies, developed an interactive program for the Internet, Virtual Spectator, to better broadcast the regattas. This allowed spectators to virtually follow as many as five matches simultaneously or replay earlier matches.

The hull of the *Young America* cracked during the second round robin, on November 9, 1999, and the crew abandoned the vessel, which nearly sank. This misadventure cast doubt on the seaworthiness of their second boat, which was making creaking sounds, and they resigned themselves to withdrawing from the Louis Vuitton Cup.

THE FINALS PLAYED OUT BETWEEN LUNA ROSSA AND *AMERICAONE* IN A MEMORABLE SERIES OF REGATTAS.

The third round robin saw the return of the Japanese sailboat *Nippon* as well as American Dawn Riley's *America True* and the French *6ᵉ Sens,* which had somehow managed to limp into the semifinals. The finals played out between *Luna Rossa* and *AmericaOne* in a memorable series of regattas, which Francesco de Angelis finally won 5 to 4.

In terms of boat design, the thirtieth America's Cup was played out between Laurie Davidson for the defense, and Doug Peterson for the challengers. The philosophies of each could be summed up as "more dynamic length" for the first, and "never slow down" for the latter. Davidson was able to gain nearly eight inches of waterline length in front with his innovative "knuckle" bow design, and the *Team New Zealand* also gained speed with its innovative three-spreader "millennium rig," with double diagonal stays in an X pattern. Russell Coutts put in a performance equaling that of 1995, which allowed him the luxury of letting his young helmsman-in-training, Dean Barker, take the helm for the last regatta. The team trounced *Luna Rossa,* 5 to 0.

There was one notable absentee: for the very first time, America was not represented in the America's Cup 2000!

USA58
YAHOO!

A view from the tactician's seat
onboard the French boat *6*^{e} *Sens* chasing the *Young America* past the Rangitoto Volcano, the symbol of Auckland.
Photograph by Gilles Martin-Raget

Almost ten years after the birth of the America's Cup Class, the research and innovative thinking of hydrodynamic engineers had concentrated on the design of these boats' keels and their famous fins. These appendages, weighing about twenty tons, are tested in a wind tunnel, often at full life scale. After a few false starts and audacious experiments, studies have been concentrated on the most classical option—as in this photograph, with a fairly low center of gravity, without being too flat—and on varying the length of the bulb and the position of the fins. A long, narrow bulb gives a larger wet surface (and thus less drag) but a smaller midsection than a short, thick bulb. This choice affects the longitudinal balance of the boat. An elongated bulb tends to make a boat more stable by keeping its center of gravity down, while a short one can allow abrupt movements, which can slow a boat down. The position of the fins depends on what effect the design team is trying to achieve. Placed far back on the bulb, they diminish drag, while in the middle, they lessen drift at the front of the boat. Their position also plays a role in stabilizing pitch. Their size varies, but they cannot exceed the maximum width of the boat.

Photograph by Gilles Martin-Raget

Significant advances had also been made in rigging design.
In their constant quest to make everything else lighter so they can increase the weight of the keel, and thus the power of the boat, boat designers had pared rigging weight down to, and sometimes beyond, the limits of known strength, as witness the tremendous number of tears and breaks during the 2000 Louis Vuitton Cup.
Photograph by Christian Février

Shades of the sinking of the *oneAustralia* in 1995 off San Diego: on November 9, 1999, at the last buoy, the *Young America* was three lengths in front of the *Asura,* the Japanese ACC boat helmed by Peter Gilmour. The American boat did a U-turn and found itself face to face with two steep, high waves. The helmsman, Ed Baird, could not prevent the boat from sliding down from the first wave to crash forcefully into the second. A crack was heard, and the boat broke in two like a jackknife, just behind the mast. First the crew abandoned ship for the lifeboat, always close; then, after they were sure that the water level had stabilized, they reboarded and attempted to save as much as they could, frantically transferring sails and equipment off the boat. The boat was filled with buoys and pumps installed to keep it afloat, then the support crew towed it back to base. The *Asura* finished the race alone. For the next race, *Young America* used its second boat, reinforced in the place where the first broke, but it never regained its standing in the competition. Second in the first round robin, it came in seventh in the next two and did not make it to the semifinals, eliminated by the French team.

Photograph by Christian Février

The day after that incident, the wind was too strong, and the ACCs remained at port. The following day, the *Asura,* the boat of Nippon Challenge, broke its mast. The wind died down for three days, and then picked up again to an acceptable limit.

November 17, with the valleys between waves as deep as six feet, was a day of disaster: seven boats were disabled by various accidents and malfunctions. Just ten minutes before its start, the Swiss *be hAPpy* abandoned the race. One of its hulls—it was the only ACC boat there with two hulls—made a cracking sound.

Mainsails tore off, spinnakers exploded. The Hawaiian *Abracadabra,* with John Kolius at the helm, broke its boom in an involuntary jibe, captured by a photographer (above).

Photograph by Gilles Martin-Raget.

ITA 45
ITA 45
PRADA

A real street brawl:
the battle between the *Luna Rossa* and the *AmericaOne* in the pounding wind during the Louis Vuitton finals remains an epic chapter of the Cup's modern history. Paul Cayard was the favorite, but Francesco de Angelis, a strikingly gentle, elegant man on land, proved to be tenacious and a very aggressive skipper at sea. To everyone's surprise, during the seventh and final regatta, he won the distinguished honor reserved for the victor of the Louis Vuitton Cup: a chance to meet the America's Cup defender.
Photograph by Gilles Martin-Raget

The ultimate victory of the *Luna Rossa*
was all the more exciting for the fact that it had been so long in doubt. On his very first attempt at the Cup, Patrizio Bertelli had won the Louis Vuitton Cup and taken a first step toward realizing his dream. A few seconds after having received the trophy from Yves Carcelle, he was already using it as a champagne bucket!
Photograph by Carlo Borlenghi/Sea & See/DPPI

COWES 2001

For every sailing enthusiast,
the August 2001 celebration of the America's Cup Jubilee at Cowes was an unmissable event.
(Preceding spread) The week of regattas, organized by the Louis Vuitton team, gathered the most beautiful boats in the Cup's history in the very place where the America's Cup myth was born in 1851.
Photograph by Philip Plisson/Pêcheur d'images

Among more than two hundred contestants
were five J-class yachts brought together for the first time.
(Above) The massive sail of the recently restored *Shamrock V* casts a shadow on the Solent as the boat lists.
Photograph by Philip Plisson/Pêcheur d'images

Chapter 7
BRUNO TROUBLÉ

The America's Cup Jubilee at Cowes: An Unforgettable Moment for a Generation of Sailors

No jubilee better lived up to its name! The week of regattas organized in August 2001 to celebrate the 150th anniversary of the America's Cup was truly a moment for jubilation.

His Majesty Juan Carlos wouldn't dream of missing such a beautiful opportunity to compete with his Farr 51. Here he is at the helm of his latest boat, the *Bribon,* a Judel-Vrolijk 54, in the MedCup 2008.
Photograph courtesy of MedCup

Those who were present will remember the details all their lives as a succession of luminous images. As for those who weren't, like Paul Cayard, they will never forgive themselves. But one thing is sure: the whole world, or close enough, was there! Not only the people who have made sailing what it is for the past two or three generations—from Russell Coutts to Olin Stephens, Alan Bond, Bill Ficker ("is quicker..."), and Ellen MacArthur—but also the most prestigious boats, from an exact replica of the *America* to the famous New Zealand *Black Magic* and Gianni Agnelli's *Stealth,* overall winner of the race around the Isle of Wight, following the same course as the historic race of August 22, 1851—the race that created the legend. Also present were the magnificent *Tuiga,* King Juan Carlos's *IMS 50 Bribon,* and the *Australia II,* which left its Australian museum for the first time since its victory in 1983 to be in Cowes.

One would love to be able to recount all the boats and men that passed before the onlookers' incredulous eyes as they swept past the Royal Yacht Squadron and its police cannon. On top of it all, the wind—not too weak, not too strong—was perfect, and a resplendent sun such as had never been seen before in Cowes shone the whole week. In brief, the event was a miracle. All the gods came together to bless this celebration of the grand old lady that is the America's Cup, in a majestic and amicable way, without a shadow of an incident—no collisions, no complaints, few beachings, no disappointment or bitterness. It was a charmed moment, only too brief—fifteen days before September 11, and a few months before Sir Peter Blake would be murdered on the Amazon. Another century, another era.

Louis Vuitton played a considerable role in organizing this historic gathering. The year before, its partners, the Royal Yacht Squadron and the New York Yacht Club, had been leaning toward canceling. The English group were hardly enthusiastic over the idea of being part of an event that, as journalist Bob Fisher put it, summarized one hundred and fifty disastrous years for British sailing competition.

The Louis Vuitton team desperately sought to persuade the squadron, which then successfully convinced the rest of the yachting world to embark on this unique festival. The company transported more than one hundred racing boats from the United States and the Mediterranean, while a liner anchored in the Solent filled in for the lack of

hotels. In the evenings, thousands of sailors and champions wandered the high street, a little tipsy with the festivities.

An Amazing Feat!

Though everything went by so quickly that week, the memorial race, run on a steady southwest wind, was incontestably the most photographed by the journalists, above all the start of the thirty-five 12-meter boats—such a fleet as had never been brought together before!—and those of the J-class, the *Velsheda,* the *Endeavour,* the *Shamrock,* and the very beautiful *Cambria,* the old reconfigured 23-meter.

The Moët dance at the Osborne House and the winning bid by Bill Koch of $450,000 for thirty-one bottles of Hennessy cognac, their vintages corresponding to the races of the America's Cup, was a great moment. As was the sight of King Juan Carlos dancing until two in the morning during the Vuitton party, accompanied by his bodyguards, forced to dance alone, not far from him, and having a hard time keeping up....

Only the *Stealth,* as black as the schooner *America,* came purely to win, putting a triumphant point on the series of Agnelli victories, a few years before the death of "l'Avvocato." The others were not really in it for the regatta results—that wasn't what this particular event was about. The essential aspect was simply to be present, to help write this wonderful page of sailing history.

Without a doubt, the festivities will start again, at the same place, to celebrate the 200th anniversary of the grand old lady of yacht races, and Louis Vuitton will again be there!

Kenny Read, skipper of the *Stealth,*
exclaimed on August 22, 2001 that there is no other word than grandiose to describe the fantastic sailing conditions, feeling like a day on the Mediterranean. He had just won the race around the Isle of Wight in 4 hours and 48 minutes. Gianni Agnelli's sailboat, a 90-footer made of carbon and conceived by German Frers, was primarily pitted against the *Mari-Cha III,* longer by 50 feet.
Photograph by Philip Plisson/Pêcheur d'images

AUCKLAND 2003

The *Alinghi* leading the dance ahead of the *Oracle BMW*
(preceding spread) in yet another image of the constant American defeats since 1995, despite three defenders and eight challenges.
Photograph by Franck Socha

It is not unusual for a spinnaker to tear.
(Above) If the crew reacts quickly enough and raise another spinnaker immediately, this kind of incident can remain harmless; if not, it can lead to catastrophe.
Photograph by Franck Socha

Chapter 8

The Swiss Take Both Cups Back to Europe

In 2003, the Swissman Ernesto Bertarelli recruited Russell Coutts, Brad Butterworth, and four other New Zealanders, winners of the two preceding America's Cup, for his brand-new challenger, the *Alinghi.* In the first round robin, two American challengers, the *OneWorld* and the *Oracle BMW,* and the Italian *Luna Rossa* demonstrated that the Swiss team was not invincible, but Alinghi polished their strategy until it was as fine-tuned as a Swiss watch, and won the Louis Vuitton Cup. Even though Team New Zealand broke new ground with its "hula" hull appendage, it suffered from the loss of the team's greatest talents, and the remaining crew's lack of experience. The *Alinghi* won the America's Cup, finally bringing the cup back to Europe after 152 years of absence.

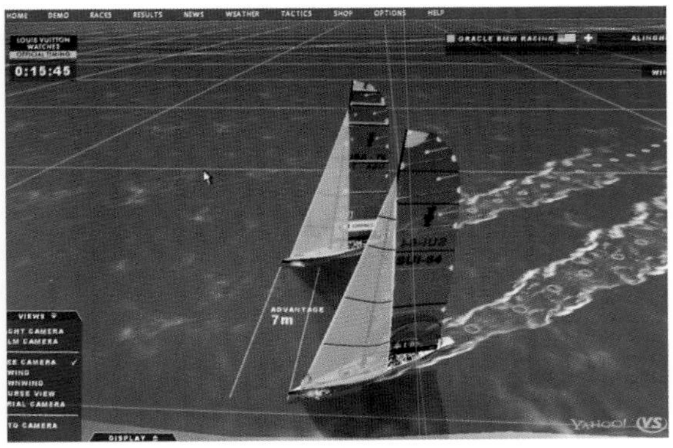

"Virtual Spectator"
is a software graphics program available on CD-ROM; anyone with a computer that can reproduce a digital image and has Internet access can now view and understand everything about a regatta, following up to five races at a time.
Photograph by Carlo Borlenghi/Sea & See/DPPI

With its history marked by intrigues, the America's Cup is a living legend. Defenders will stop at nothing to hold on to it. The America's Cup had appeared to be secure in New Zealand for a long time to come, as the team seemed so far ahead of the challengers. Still, things were a little murkier at the heart of the Team New Zealand Syndicate. After his double victory, Sir Peter Blake, having decided to give up racing and instead devote himself to scientific expeditions, had yielded his place as syndicate director to Russell Coutts and Brad Butterworth. But after the tragic death of Blake in the Amazon, the two men came up against passive resistance from the team's financial backers, who refused to let them in on decisions regarding the defense of the 31st America's Cup. So when he met up in New York with the Swiss businessman Ernesto Bertarelli, who was thinking of launching his own challenge, Russell felt free to accept his offer to join. Soon Brad Butterworth—along with other New Zealand team members, including tactician Murray Jones, Simon Daubney, Dean Phipps, and Warwick Fleury—joined him. The German Jochen Schumann, the Australian Grant Simmer, the Dutch architect Rolf Vrolijk, and a few specialists of diverse nationalities completed a crew that proved from the start to be formidable.

For America's Cup 2003, ten yacht clubs issued a challenge to the Royal New Zealand Yacht Club—six from Europe, three from the United States, and one from Japan. The selection process for the participants of the Louis Vuitton Cup, which began on October 1, 2002, had been modified: there were only two round robins, but repechage series were added to both quarterfinals and semifinals to give those who had lost in the first round a second chance. The results and scorekeeping were still centralized, as in 1995, at the Louis Vuitton Media Center, and instant communiqués were sent by the Louis Vuitton staff directed by Bruno Troublé. Henceforth, Louis Vuitton Watches would be the official timekeeper of the Louis Vuitton Cup.

Prada Challenge returned with the same crew and two new *Luna Rossa* sailboats. Regarded as favorites at the start, they were soon reduced to a token role in the selections, up to the semifinals. The ousting of Doug Peterson from their design team in the first round robin created a malaise that could not improve their results. The second Italian challenger, *Mascalzone Latino,* was led by the likable owner Vincenzo Onorato, who was also the boat's helmsman. Though its name meant "Latin rascal," *Mascalzone Latino* fought above all for its survival. It won only a single victory, against *FRA 69* of Le Défi Areva, and was the first to leave the round robin.

Sweden had been absent since 1992 from the Vuitton Cup, even though they were the first nation to launch a challenge to the schooner *America,* in 1852. Jan Stenbeck, owner of a television studio and of the newspaper *Metro,* took up the venture. He died

THE FRENCH CHALLENGER WAS DECIDEDLY PROVOCATIVE. THE SAIL NUMBER ON THEIR BOAT, *FRA 69,* RAN IN THE SAME VEIN OF HUMOR AS THE NAME OF THEIR *FRENCH KISS* IN 1987.

of a heart attack two weeks before the racing, but his son Hugo and his crew members took up the torch. The Swedish boat *Örn* battled honorably, earning seven points. Victorious in the quarterfinals against *FRA 69* of Le Défi Areva, it fell to the *Luna Rossa ITA 80* in the repechage matches.

Peter Harrison's GBR Challenge was distinguished by its originality. Harrison had already bought the three *Nippon* boats used for Japan's unsuccessful 2000 challenge and entered two of them in the 2001 America's Cup Jubilee fleet race; he recruited the New Zealander David Barnes and an exclusive crew of the most talented English sailors of the younger generation. The most surprising was his position as "seventeenth man" (the extra position on board reserved for a guest) onboard his *Wight Lightning GBR 70,* where he sat in a plastic lawn chair in a rear cockpit especially constructed for him. Tied with the *Stars & Stripes USA 66* by the end of the round robin, he was quickly dispatched by his adversary in the quarterfinals.

The French challenger was decidedly provocative. The sail number on their boat, *FRA 69,* which the British had refused to take when it was assigned to them, ran in the same vein of humor as the name of their *French Kiss* in 1987; they were sponsored by the nuclear power company Areva (the name of their team), stirring up memories of the notorious *Rainbow Warrior* affair. Their fluorescent yellow hull was hard to miss in the bright sun of Hauraki Bay. The challenger was eliminated in the quarterfinals, but if their race results were disappointing, their publicity campaign obviously succeeded.

Dennis Conner was still there, with his *Stars & Stripes,* his friends Tom Whidden, Bill Trenkle, and Ken Read at the helm, once again representing the New York Yacht Club. While training off the coast of San Diego, his newest boat sank over fifty feet to the bottom due to a rudder break. Bailed out, Dennis's fighting spirit stayed intact, and he arrived in time for the beginning of the Louis Vuitton Cup, but remained an outsider and was beaten four times by the *OneWorld USA 65* in the repechage series in the quarterfinals.

The two other American challengers were strong, directed by the men who had made their fortune in new technologies on the East Coast of the United States. Craig McCaw, under the banner of the Seattle Yacht Club, director of OneWorld Challenge, acquired the winning design team of Laurie Davidson and Bruce Nelson, and chose Peter Gilmour and James Spithill as helmsmen. Even if Craig met with a few financial difficulties, the *OneWorld* possessed the advantage of having trained five months in two IACC races. He won eight matches in the first round robin, lost four against the *Oracle BMW USA 76* in the quarterfinals, dropped Dennis Conner in the repechage, and beat the *Luna Rossa ITA 94* in the semifinals 4 to 2, but was squashed 4 to 0 in the following series, once again at the hands of the *Oracle BMW.*

RUSSELL COUTTS WON A RECORD OF FOURTEEN OUT OF FOURTEEN AMERICA'S CUP RACES SINCE 1995.

Larry Ellison had Bruce Farr design the two *Oracle BMW* sister ships—which were magnificent and, although not unusual, certainly also as fast as the three best IACC boats in the Louis Vuitton Cup—and recruited Paul Cayard, John Cutler, Chris Dickson, and Peter Holmberg, who teamed up in the afterguard. Ellison wanted to be an active part of the crew, saying, "I'm absolutely going to drive the boat, as long as it won't hurt the team." He even dreamed of modifying the rules so that owners would be obliged to take the helm. But the America's Cup is not the place for amateur yachtsmen, and tension quickly rose within the team. Both Cayard and Cutler left; Ellison decided to step off the boat, and Holmberg and Dickson shared the helm. The *Oracle BMW USA 76* was beaten 4 to 0 in the semifinals, then 5 to 1 in the final of the Louis Vuitton Cup by the *Alinghi SUI 64.*

Although his boat's "hula" hull appendage, meant to lengthen the waterline, was intriguing, Dean Barker was not able to prove that the *Team New Zealand* was faster for it. In stronger than usual winds and sometimes choppy waters, Russell Coutts, with Alinghi America's Cup 2003, won five races in a row in the finals to claim the America's Cup—giving him a record of fourteen out of fourteen America's Cup races won since 1995.

After 152 years, the cup would finally return to Europe.

Auckland is not the capital of New Zealand, but it is by far the largest city in the country. Sailing vies with rugby as the national sport, and each day, thousands of spectators followed each leg of the races.

The Louis Vuitton Cup flag flew for weeks above the Harbor Bridge, next to the national flag. On the left, beyond the second basin, one can see the challengers' bases along the Viaduct Harbor. Prada Challenge is farthest to the left. The Louis Vuitton Media Center is situated under the long white roof on the far left. The sun is here to the north, while the wind blows from the south.

Photograph by Bob Grieser

Alinghi easily defeated American competitor Oracle BMW Racing
in the final of the Louis Vuitton Cup. Here we see *Oracle BMW* approaching the buoy upwind: The 600-square-meter spinnaker is furled, ready to be raised in a few seconds. The ball visible at the back of the boat is one of the four remote-controlled cameras mounted on each boat in competition.
Photograph by Franck Socha

The *Wight Lighting GBR 70* and the *Luna Rossa ITA 74* going head-to-head
soon after the start of the race: The two boats were only apart by a few yards, the outcome of the race still totally uncertain. Francesco de Angelis and the *Luna Rossa* eventually won every round robin, though David Barnes lost by less than half a minute each time, sixteen seconds the first and twenty-two the second. He was finally eliminated in the quarterfinals by the *Stars & Stripes USA 77,* 5 to 1.
Photograph by Carlo Borlenghi/Sea & See/DPPI

Triple America's Cup winner Dennis Conner,
back for his last Cup with the *Stars & Stripes*: His new boat, still the same "gunsmoke" blue, was not very competitive and was eliminated before the semifinals of the Louis Vuitton Cup. Here we see him ahead of the GBR Challenge boat. During the second round robin, he dropped to his lowest score, finishing second to last of the challengers, tied with the *FRA 69* of Le Défi Areva.
Photograph by Franck Socha

ORACLE

In radio contact with the tactician,
the strategist climbs to the masthead to attempt to analyze the wind, anticipate its mood swings, and inform the crew. This new technique has become widespread since the 2000 Louis Vuitton Cup.
Photograph by Carlo Borlenghi/Sea & See/DPPI

UBS
AUDEMARS PIGUET

Happy days:
The best skipper in the world—who did not lose a regatta over three editions of the America's Cup (1995, 2000, and 2003)—scored a victory for Switzerland. He celebrated his triumph with Ernesto Bertarelli, the man behind the *Alinghi*. The Moët champagne was flowing. A few months later, these two headstrong individuals had a sudden falling-out.
Photograph by Carlo Borlenghi/Sea & See/DPPI

VALENCIA 2007

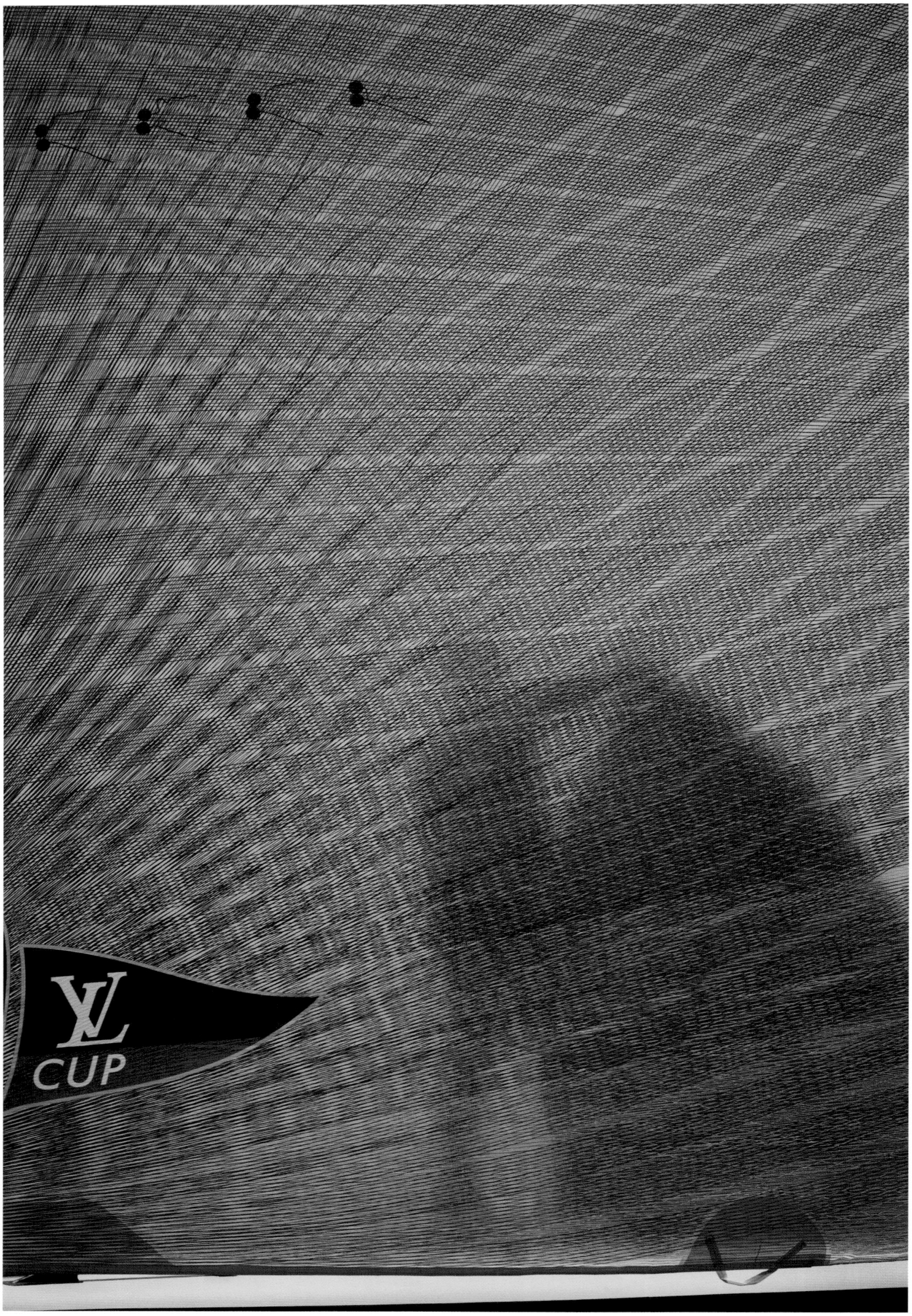

An aesthetically pleasing
(preceding spread) and informative photograph: the upper part of the jib is opened to direct effective airflow to the belly of the mainsail.
Photograph by Franck Socha

Translucent modern sails,
which are made by combining various films and fibers—Kevlar, carbon, Mylar—lend themselves to surprising photographic images: (Above) Here a shadow-puppet crewman prepares a new sail on the deck beyond the sail.
Photograph by Philip Plisson/Pêcheur d'images

Chapter 9

From Marseille to Valencia: Three Years of Racing for a New Swiss Victory

The America's Cup had finally come to Europe. Between 2004 and 2007, eleven challengers from nine different countries battled in thirteen Louis Vuitton Acts and one Louis Vuitton Cup in Marseille, Malmö, Trapani, and Valencia, in both match and fleet races, with and without the defender, for the right to meet the *Alinghi.*

The rules were completely changed, Louis Vuitton was no longer the sole sponsor of the Louis Vuitton Cup, and the defender would be present at all levels of the organization and the coverage of the event. The rule that defined the sailboats was modified, standardizing the principal characteristics of the America's Cup Class.

The Kiwis won the Louis Vuitton Cup for the second time, but were vanquished by the *Alinghi* in the America's Cup.

Emirates Team New Zealand eliminated Luna Rossa Challenge 5 to 0 in the finals. Yves Carcelle presenting Dean Barker and Grant Dalton with the Louis Vuitton Cup.
Photograph by Antoine Jarrier/Archives Louis Vuitton

Has the silver cup become cursed? Alan Bond, after 1983, became a megalomaniac, buying extravagantly expensive Impressionist paintings that he really couldn't afford. Michael Fay was on the brink of victory in 1987; the next year, he launched his deliriously grand "Big Boat" challenge. And the New Zealand syndicate, once it had the Cup secure in Auckland in 2000, seemed to believe it could do without sailors....

In 2003, the Swiss businessman Ernesto Bertarelli was admired by the entire sports community. Winner of his first challenge, he had brought together a good crew and a fine boat with the *Alinghi.* By serving as a crew member on his boat, he had assured his place; it was an exemplary gesture. But during the first press conference, he announced his intention of directing the America's Cup his own way.

AC Management, a direct offshoot of the Alinghi defense syndicate, would completely control the America's Cup—its rules, its interests, the challenger selections, and the defense. As it was not possible to organize the event on Lake Geneva, four European cities—Marseille, Malmö, Trapani, and Valencia—were considered. The competition for the honor of hosting the upcoming festivities created such feverish bidding that it ultimately created friction between the *Alinghi* skipper Russell Coutts and the management, which resulted in the ousting of Coutts.

In September 2003, Larry Ellison, on the *BMW Oracle,* invited the *Alinghi* to a regatta on its home waters, in the San Francisco Bay, for the Moët Cup. He organized owners' regattas and finally tasted victory over Bertarelli, as they each were at the helm of their own America's Cup Class yacht. The following June, in Newport, on an invitation from Alinghi in the UBS Trophy, he repeated his performance.

Finally, Valencia, Spain, was chosen as the host city for the 2007 America's Cup. The entry fee was raised by a considerable amount for the first time in the long history of the trophy. A program for the preliminary rounds was established, with match and fleet races counting toward the selections for the challengers.

During the early racing, the competitors—including the defenders in the selection regattas—sailed with 2000- or 2003-generation IACCs. The rule formula was now stricter, allowing almost no leeway in waterline length, sail surface, and displacement. Thus, architects had to concentrate on hull width and form and the balance between the elements of boat design.

The selections program provided for thirteen Louis Vuitton Acts between 2004 and 2007. The odd-numbered acts were fleet regattas; the even ones were match races. At the end of those matches two round robins, semifinals, and finals for the Louis Vuitton

STARTING THE BEGINNING OF ACT 4, IN JUNE 2005, THE OLD IACC YACHTS BEGAN TO BE MODIFIED TO MEET THE STANDARDS OF THE NEW RULE.

Cup continued up to the month of June. Louis Vuitton, who had developed a new line of watches in the past two years, was again the official timekeeper of the event.

The Louis Vuitton Acts began in Marseille. Six of twelve competitors were present for four fleet races. South Africa's *Shosholoza* was not only the first America's Cup Class yacht to be designed and built in South Africa, but the first in the world to meet the new rule. Three teams took the first three places: BMW Oracle Racing, Alinghi, and Emirates Team New Zealand. The two French challengers, *K-Challenge* and *Le Défi,* still looking for sponsors, placed before Team Shosholoza. By the end of the Marseille regattas, however, a violent storm had descended on the base, crushing the top three sailboats against the quay.

The following month, eight IACC yachts confronted one another in Valencia for Acts 2 and 3: two Italians, the *Luna Rossa* and the *+39,* were the largest of the fleet. The *Team New Zealand* and the *Alinghi* arrived in the lead in each of the two acts; the *Luna Rossa,* with Francesco de Angelis at the helm, came in second in the first series. Dean Barker, on the *Team New Zealand,* won the 2004 series, ahead of Chris Dickson, skipper of the *BMW Oracle.*

Starting at the beginning of Act 4, in June 2005, the old IACC yachts began to be modified to meet the standards of the new rule. Two new countries entered the event: China and Germany. The businessman Chaoyang Wang and his China Team recruited French crew members, along with a few Chinese sailors. To support the spirit of the newcomer, the two cups—the America's Cup and the Louis Vuitton Cup—made a voyage to Asia and were paraded along the Wall of China. The last of the eleven challengers to be enrolled, the United Internet Team Germany sailed the *United I Team Germany,* a modification of the *Mascalzone Latino* of 2003. The three other challengers were Italian yachtsman Vincenzo Onorato's Mascalzone Latino–Capitalia Team, Swedish Victory Challenge, and the Spanish Desafío Español 2007, who were sailing in their own waters and benefited from national support.

During 2005, six series of regattas were organized, in Valencia, Malmö, and Trapani, Sicily. There was no question of moving the gigantic bases installed along the America's Cup Harbor in Valencia. Each challenger could move only one single sailboat, with two or three containers to hold sails, the rigging, and other equipment. All of the boats were lined up in front of the harbor of each city, without tarps, in full view of everyone. The crews stayed on a liner chartered for the occasion, moored at the end of the quay, creating a convivial atmosphere exceptional in the history of the America's Cup. The *Alinghi* proved to be the dominant boat that year, followed by the Kiwis' *Team New Zealand.*

THE *ALINGHI* PROVED TO BE THE DOMINANT BOAT THAT YEAR, FOLLOWED BY THE KIWIS' TEAM NEW ZEALAND.

For the last Louis Vuitton Acts, between May 2006 and April 2007, the winners remained the same, though the *BMW Oracle USA 87* won Act 10. During the two round robins that followed, from which Alinghi was absent, the three top challengers stayed in the same order: Emirates Team New Zealand, BMW Oracle Racing, and Luna Rossa Challenge, with Desafío Español 2007 taking fourth place in front of Mascalzone Latino–Capitalia Team and Victory Challenge. Seven challengers dropped out. The Kiwis, as winners, had the choice of their competitor for the semifinals, beating Desafío Español 2007, while Luna Rossa Challenge eliminated BMW Oracle Racing. In the final, Dean Barker and Emirates Team New Zealand routed the Italians 5 to 0. There had been 566 regattas to finish this Louis Vuitton Cup.

The America's Cup played out between the *Alinghi SUI 100* and the *Team New Zealand NZL 92,* same as in 2003. The *Alinghi* won 5 to 2; in the seventh and last match, just for the books, the *Alinghi* came in only one second ahead!

Although Louis Vuitton, through the years, had become synonymous with the America's Cup, on July 13, 2007, the directors of the company announced the withdrawal of their sponsorship. The America's Cup no longer seemed to represent the spirit of the company, either in its new rules, in its image, or in its values. Will this withdrawal be temporary or permanent? Only time will tell. All depends on the spirit in which future winners organize the Cup.

ZEALAND

The red spinnaker
of the *Team New Zealand* paints the water's surface scarlet. Carrying 7,000 square feet of sail, this IACC boat cuts through the water in the slightest breeze.
Photograph by Carlo Borlenghi/Sea & See/DPPI

FRA-57
FRA 69
RSA48
msc

Though Marseille didn't succeed in being appointed to host the 32nd America's Cup,
the Louis Vuitton Act 1 held in that city in September 2004 was memorable for its beautiful location and ideal racing conditions. Here the boats have just started off under the protection of "La Bonne Mère" (Notre-Dame de la Garde) and, like knife blades under the sun, they forged ahead against the wind.
Photograph by Philip Plisson/Pêcheur d'images

Participants in the Louis Vuitton Cup and the America's Cup
compete one-on-one in match races, but the Swiss organizers had the great idea of holding highly spectacular fleet regattas during the Louis Vuitton Acts that preceded the round robins: ten boats tack as one at the start of the race.
Photograph by Franck Socha

On the other side of the spectrum,
a duel can be just as photogenic, in a more artistic light. The image of two listing boats, crossing like swords, remains the quintessential symbol of the America's Cup. The New Zealand sailboat, which has the right-of-way, passes just in front of the South African one, which sticks close behind.
Photograph by Bob Grieser

USA 71
GER72
1&1
Allianz
ORACLE

The America's Cup circus
also set up camp in Kiel, Germany, in the summer of 2006. The regattas took place in the harbor where the German Optimist championships were also held. The young skippers must have been a little startled to be confronted with IACC yachts, spinnikers billowing and surging past at 13 knots. Everyone managed to avoid a collision and go home with an unforgettable memory of the day's events.
Photograph by Richard Walch

From the earliest days of the Cup,
the manoeuvering at the pre-start had always been spectacular. Each competitor circling, trying to earn the advantage while attempting to avoid attacks: a veritable ballet that lasts for several minutes. Here, the sailboats have unwittingly drawn a nearly perfect heart.
Photograph by Richard Walch

RSA48
RSA48
msc
T··Systems
SOUTH AFRICA
MEDITERRANEAN SHIPPING CO.
MSC
T··Systems
SHOSHOLOZA
ORACLE
ORACLE

ITALIA
independent ideas
trentanove

Four seconds before the start,
Dean Barker on the *Team New Zealand* picks up speed going left, while Iain Percy, aboard *+39,* opted for the right side.
Photograph by Luca Villata

With hand signals,
the bowman of the Swedish *Järv,* upwind of the Italian *+39,* conveys precise information to his skipper, Magnus Holmberg.
Photograph by Franck Socha

The French team Areva Challenge, which took part in the Louis Vuitton Cup 2000 and 2003, attended the Louis Vuitton Acts of 2004 but didn't quite have the means. An alliance with the China Team allowed the French syndicate to make their challenge a reality, the French offering their experience both on and off the water. During the winter of 2005–6, a recruitment process to integrate Chinese sailors was set up. The only serious competitor was South African Team Shosholoza, newly come to the Cup but showing remarkable progress, rapidly becoming a serious rival.

China Team did not win a single match; its best showing was ninth in the fleet regattas of Act 11. It logically then placed twelfth in its class by the end of the season. "You know, we are the smallest team, and it is very important to develop a strong image from the start of our venture, if we want to hold our own against the big publicity machines," affirmed Pierre Mas, skipper of the China Team. Certainly, with its red dragon, a historical symbol of Chinese culture, on a yellow background, the *Longtze* ("Son of the Dragon") *CHN 95* succeeded in being one of the most photographed boats in the America's Cup.

Photograph by Bob Grieser

Allianz
ORACLE
GIRARD-PERREGAUX
BMW ORACLE Racing

Chris Dickson on the *BMW Oracle USA 98* is in the lead,
but the *Team New Zealand NZL 84* attempts to pass on the starboard side. Notice the difference in the angle of the boats' mainsails; that of the *NZL 84* is pulled much closer to the boat. In the Louis Vuitton Cup finals, which rounded off some 1,490 races since 1983, Emirates Team New Zealand were able to avoid pitting themselves against this formidable opponent.
Photograph by Bob Grieser

FlyEmirates
FlyEmirates

A grand tradition:
as soon as the finish line was crossed, Yves Carcelle and Bruno Troublé boarded the winning vessel with a few bottles of Moët champagne to celebrate the victory with the crew. The New Zealand team, although still exhausted by the race, was overwhelmed with joy at that moment.
Photograph by Paul Todd/DPPI

Boat Designs

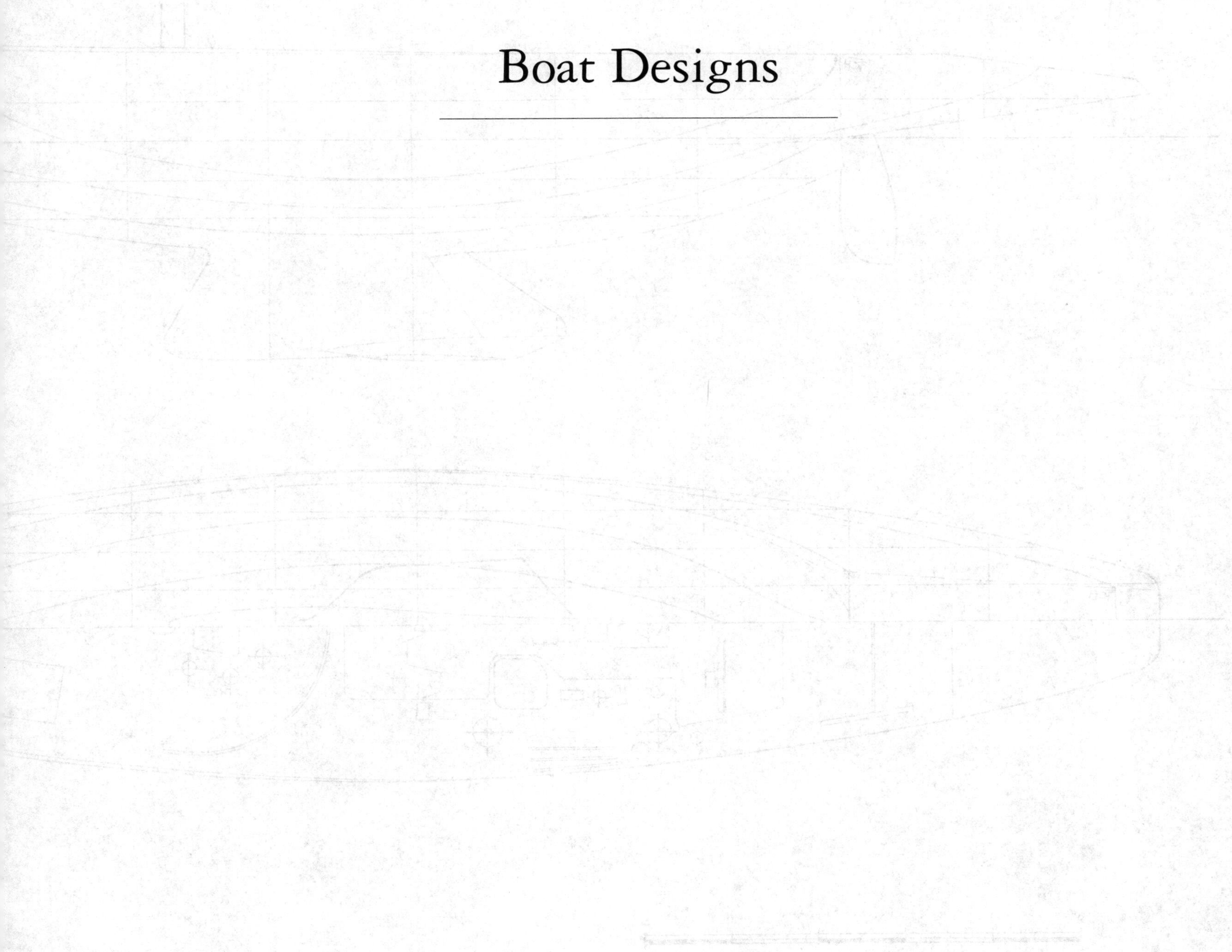

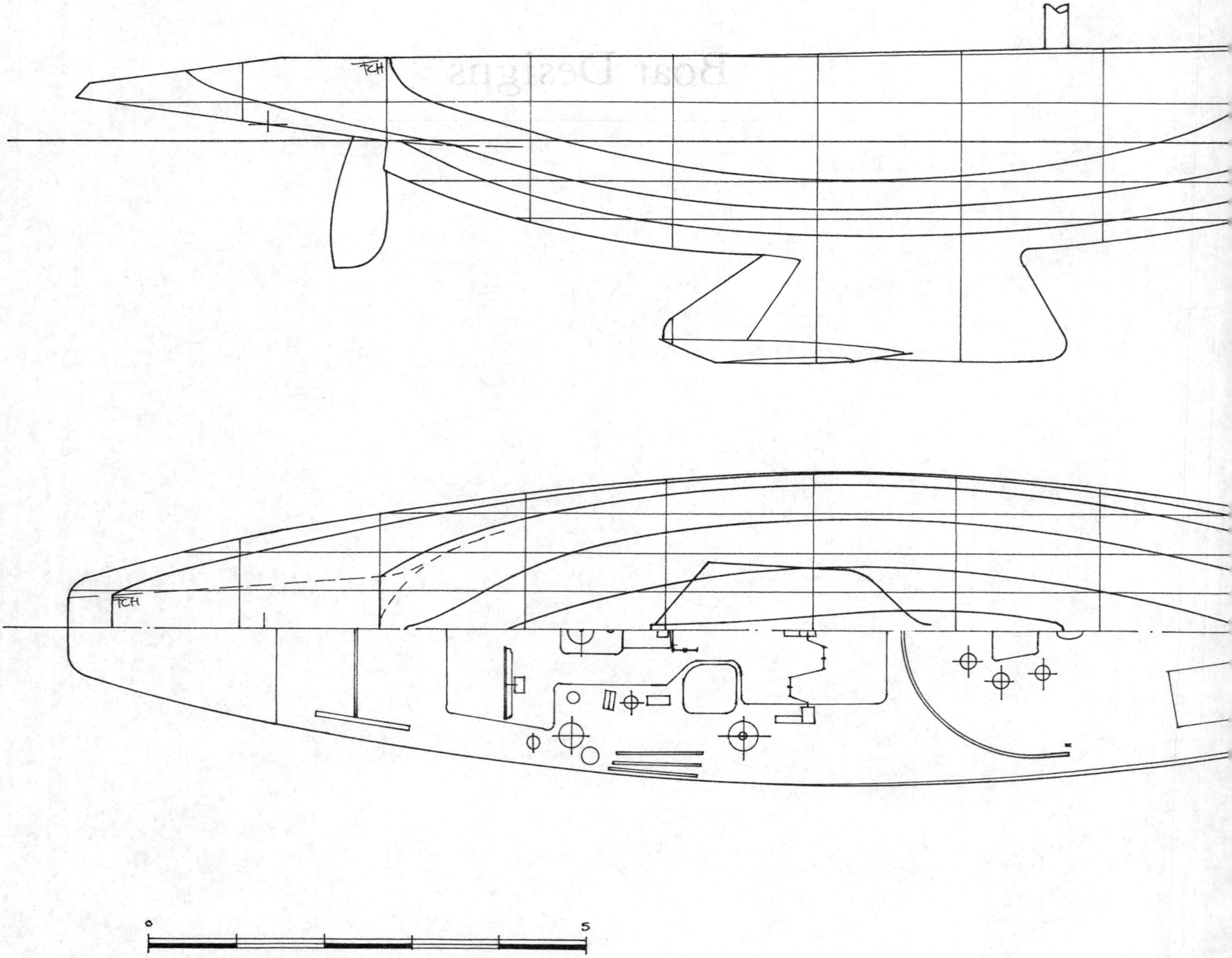
TCH
TCH
0
5

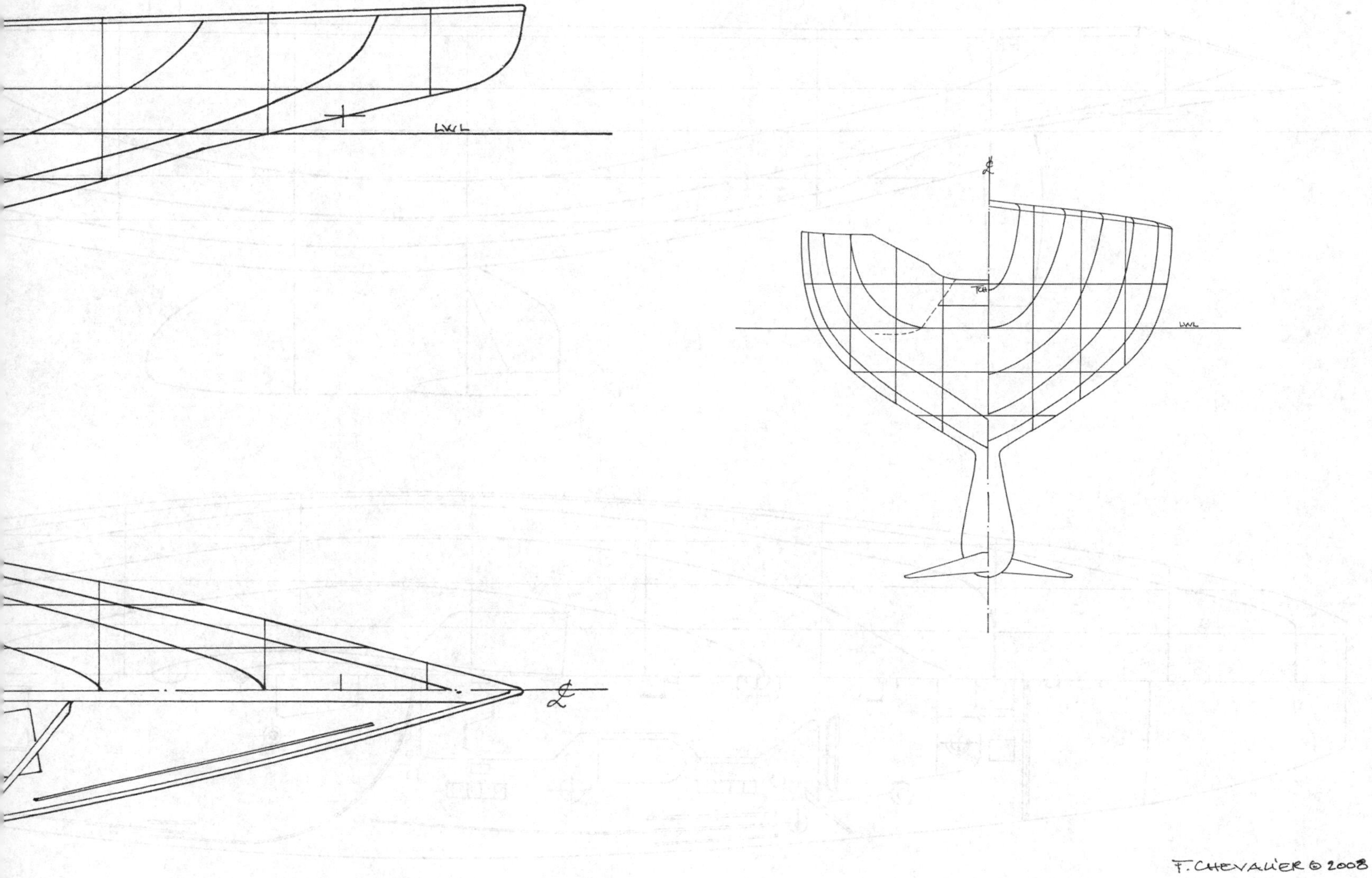

1983./ AUSTRALIA II – KA 6

Winner of the Louis Vuitton Cup, 1983, and
of the 25th America's Cup challenge in 1983
12-meter, sail number: KA 6
Australia

Yacht club: Royal Perth Yacht Club
Owner: America's Cup Challenge 1983, Alan Bond
Builder: Steve E. Ward & Co., Cottesloe, Australia
Master Sailmaker: Tom Schnackenberg, sails by North, Hood, and Sobstad, Australia
Architect: Ben Lexcen

Research center and towing tank: Netherlands Ship Model Basin, in Wageningen, the Netherlands, Peter Van Oossanen.

Models made by a third party.
Hydrodynamics: Joop W. Sloff of the Theorythical Aerodynamic Department of the National Aerospace Laboratory, Amsterdam, the Netherlands

Launch: June 3, 1982
Christening: June 6, 1982, by Eileen Bond in Fremantle

Skipper: John Bertrand
Tactician: Hugh Treharne
Navigator: Grant Simmer
Crew: 11

Specifications:
Overall length: 19.21 m
Waterline length: 13.10 m
Beam: 3.64 m
Draft: 2.59 m
Sail surface area: 175 m^2
Displacement: 21.8 tons
Hull material: aluminum

Notes: On exhibition at the National Maritime Museum in Sydney, Australia, then at the Western Australian Maritime Museum of Fremantle. Participated at Cowes, Isle of Wight, in the regattas celebrating the 150th anniversary of the America's Cup in August 2001, then returned to the museum.

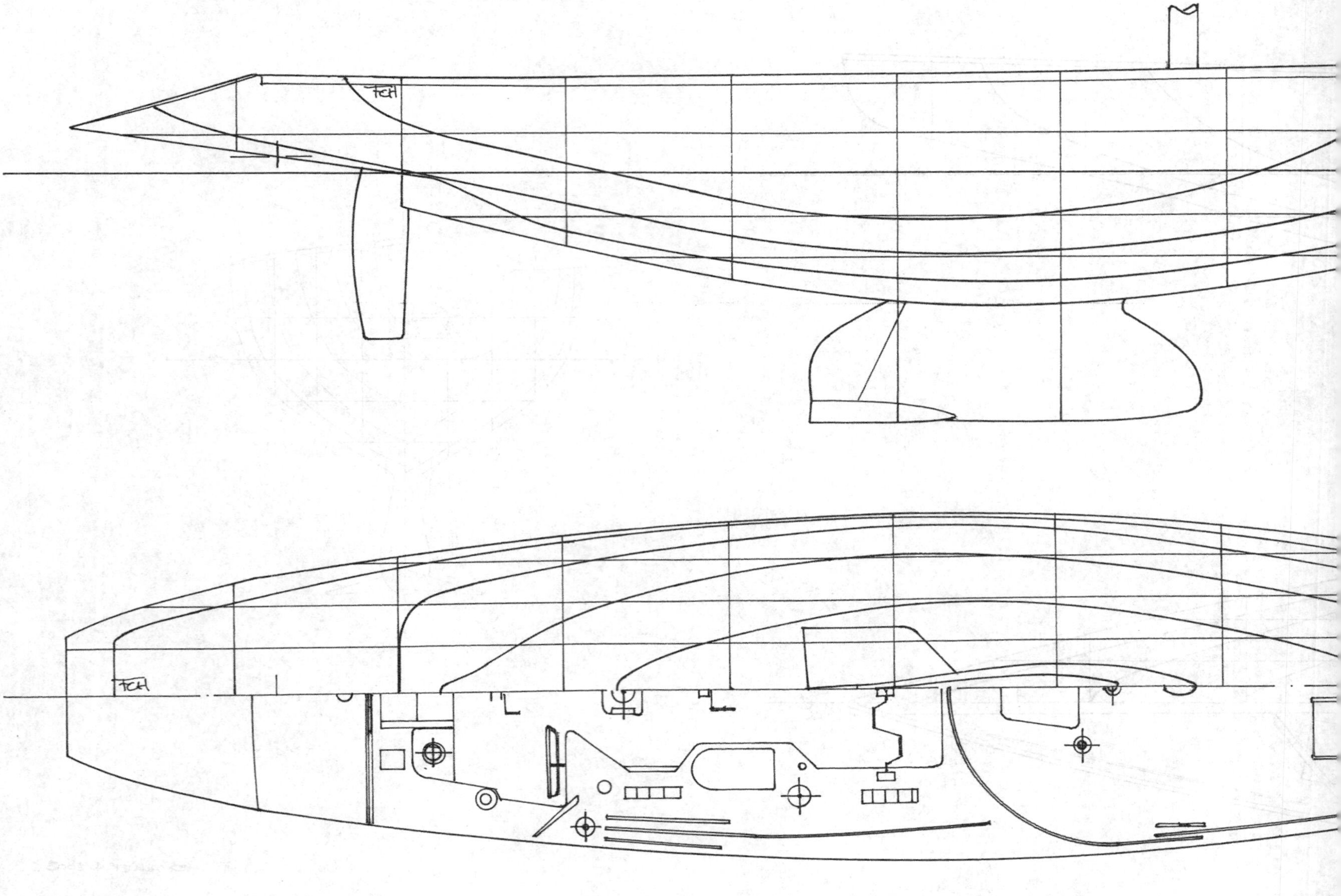
FCH
FCH
0
5

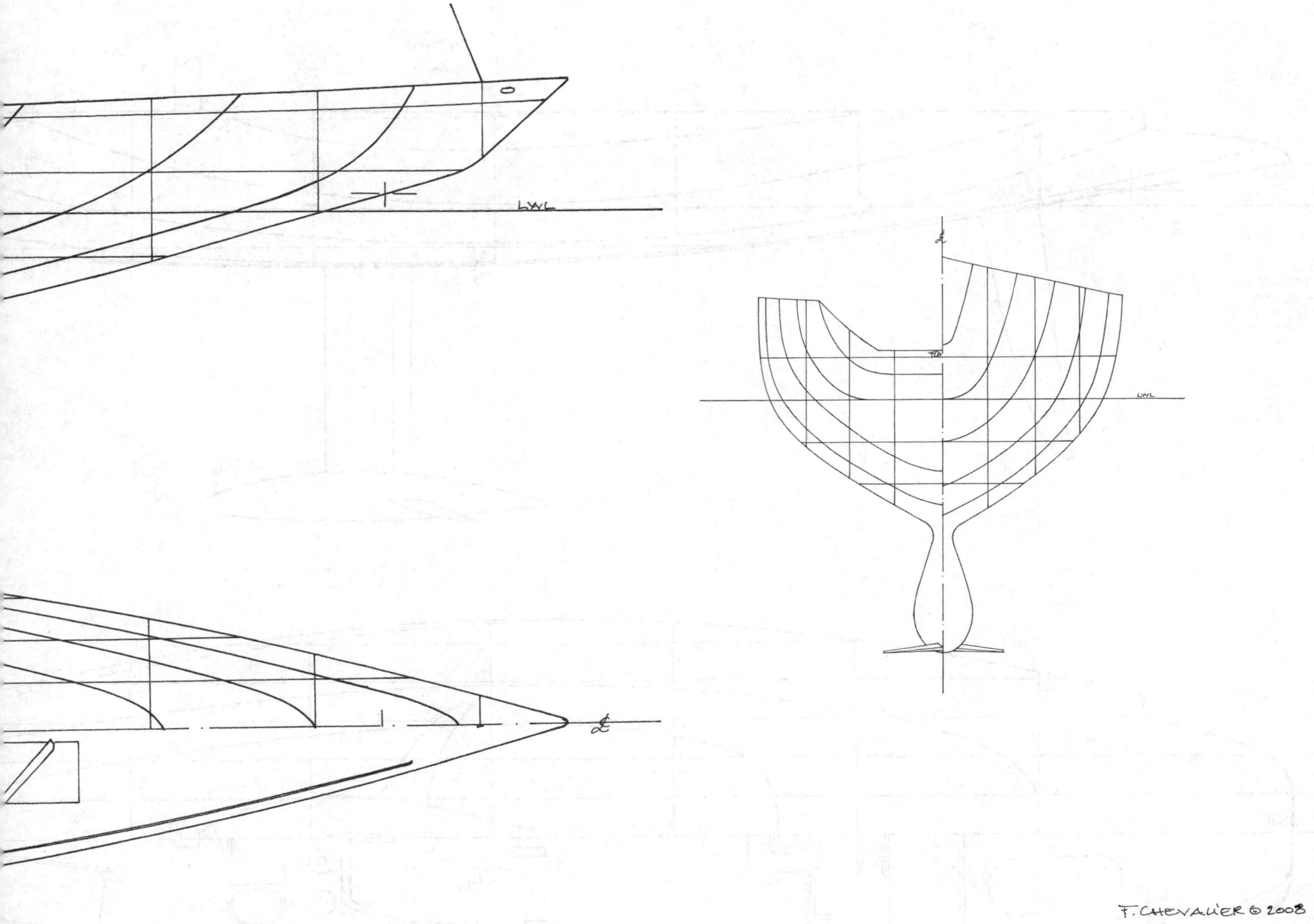

1987./ STARS & STRIPES – US 55

Winner of the Louis Vuitton Cup, 1987, and
of the 26th America's Cup challenge in 1987
12-meter, sail number: US 55
United States
Yacht club: San Diego Yacht Club

Owner: Sail America Foundation for International Understanding
President: Malin Burnham

Builder: Robert E. Derecktor, Mamaroneck, New York
Master sailmakers: Jack Stutphen, Sobstad Sails, North Sails, We Be Guessing
Coordinator: John Marshall
Architects: Britton Chance, Jr., Bruce Nelson, David Pedrick
Research centers: Science Applications International Corporation (SAIC)
Flight Research Institute of Boeing Company, Seattle
Towing tank: Offshore Technology Corporation in Escondido, California
Hydrodynamics: Grumman Aerospace, New York

Christening: July 14, 1986, at the University of Hawaii in Marine Center, in Honolulu, Hawaii

Skipper: Dennis Conner
Tactician: Tom A. Whidden
Navigator: Peter Isler
Crew: 11

Specifications:
Overall length: 20.23 m
Waterline length: 13.92 m
Beam: 3.81 m
Draft: 2.82 m
Sail surface area: 170 m²
Displacement: 28.18 tons
Hull material: aluminium

Notes: From 1988 to 1989, the America's Cup Organizing Committee owned the boat. Between 1992 and 1994, George F. Jewett, Jr. sailed the boat from his home port of San Francisco. In 1996, Dennis Conner Sports, Inc., acquired the boat, which they kept in San Diego. It then became part of the America's Cup Yacht Racing fleet in Saint Martin, in the Caribbean, where it served as a charter boat.

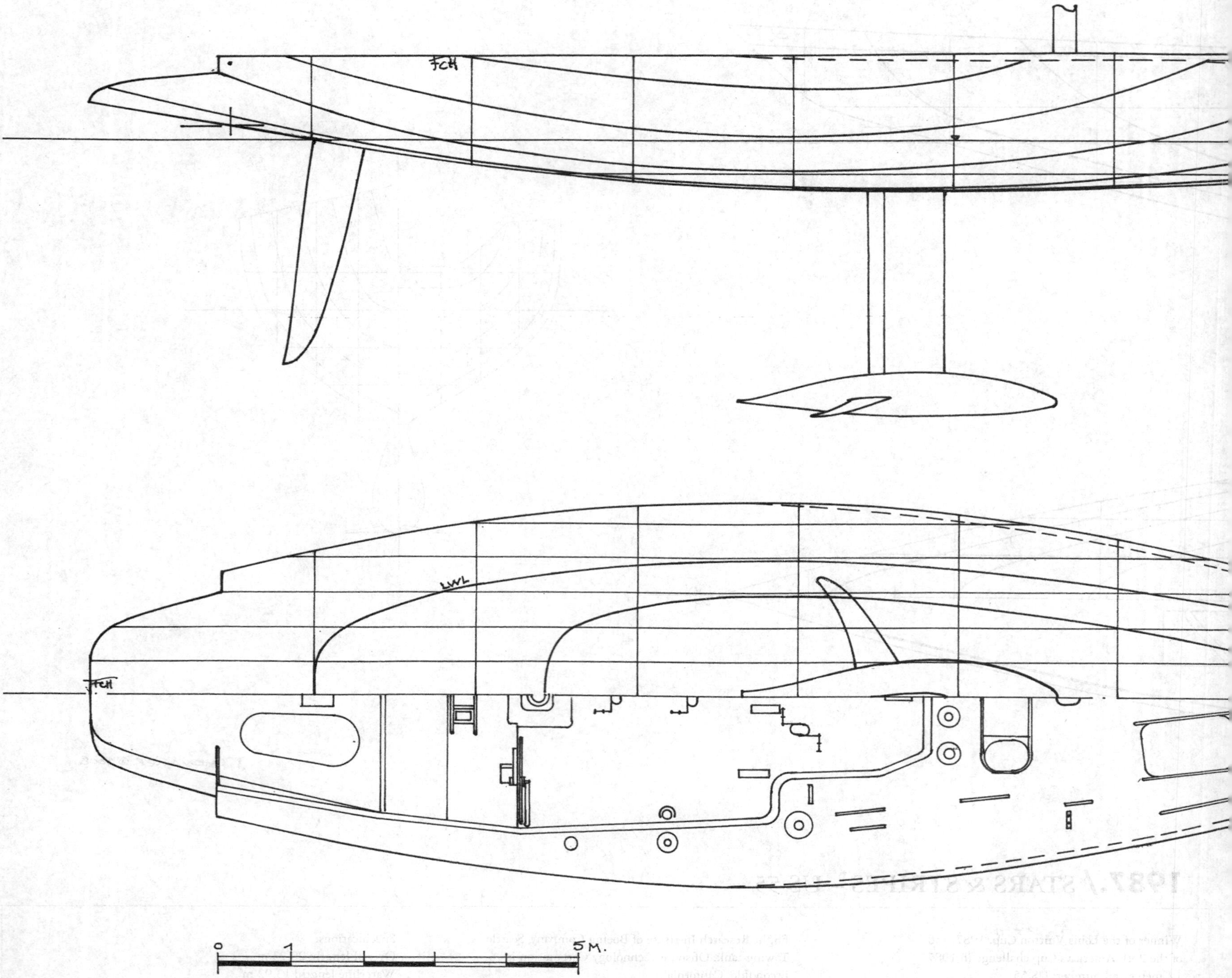
FCH
FCH
LWL
0
1
5M.

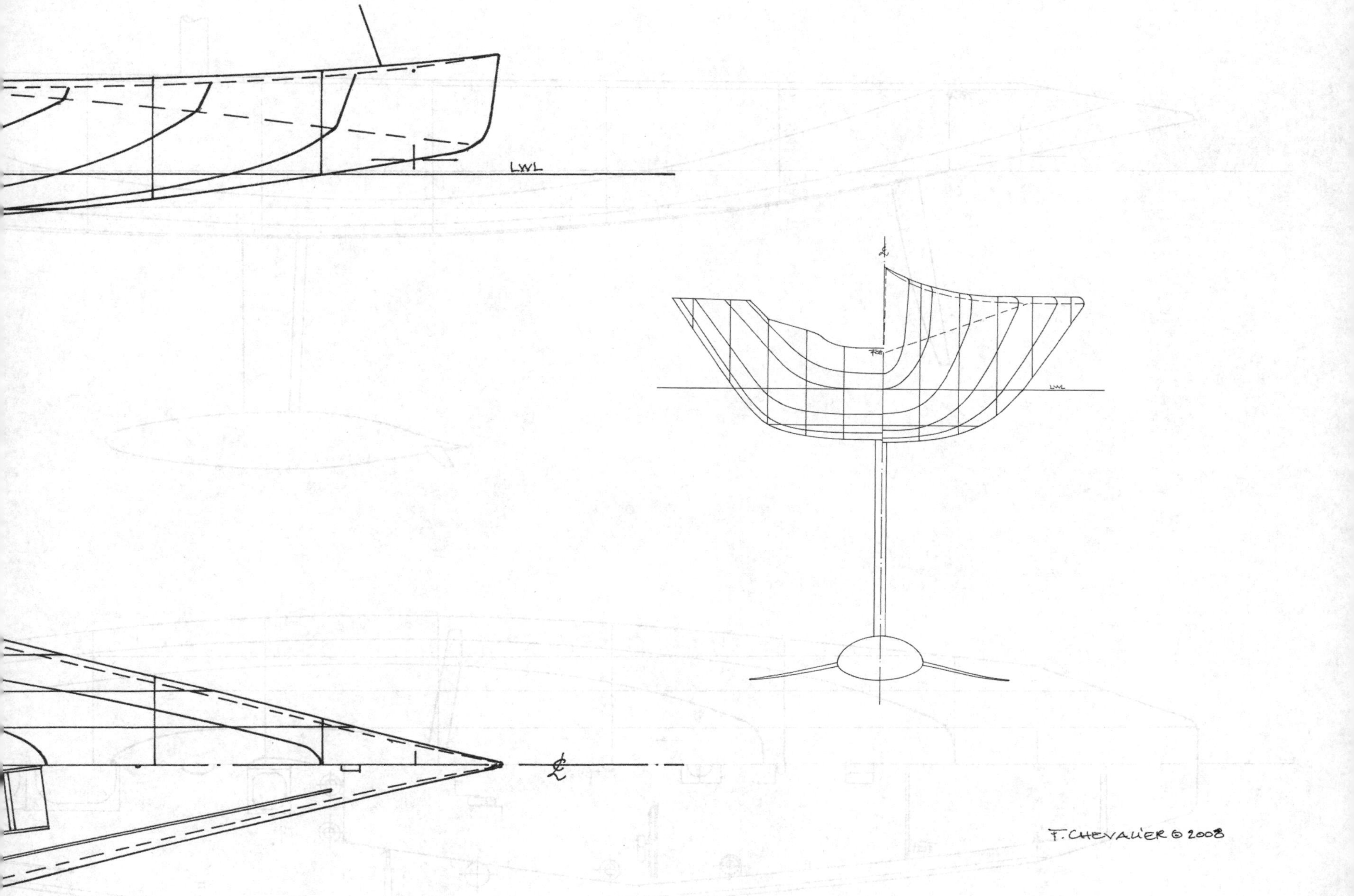

1992./ IL MORO DI VENEZIA V – ITA 25

Winner of the Louis Vuitton Cup, 1992
International America's Cup Class, sail number: ITA 25
Italy
Yacht club: Compania Della Vela Yacht Club, Venise
Commodore: Giulio Donatelli

Owner: Il Moro di Venezia Syndicate, presided over by Raul Gardini
Director General of Operations: Laurent Esquier

Builder: Tencara, Porto Marghera, near Venice, Italy
Spars and rigging: ACX and Chris Mitchell
Architect: German Frers (Argentina)
Design team: Giovanni Belgrano, Micky Costa, Nestor Fourcade, Debora Gallazzi, Claudio Maletto, Raffaele Marrazzi, Leopoldo Murcho, Francesco Ricci, Oliver Yates
Research group: Robert Hopkins, Jr. (United States)

Towing tank: INSEAN, Rome; 20 models tested
Meteorologist: Roger Badham
Sails: North Sails Italia

Launch: December 16, 1991, in San Diego

Skipper: Paul Cayard
Tactician: Tommaso Chieffi
Navigator: Enrico Chieffi/Robert Hopkins
Crew: 16 + 1
Training boat helmsmen: John Kolius, Steve Erikson

Specifications:
Overall length: 22.90 m
Waterline length: 18.10 m
Bow: 5.50 m
Draft: 4 m
Sail surface area: 326.6 m^2
Spinnaker: 425 m^2
Mast height: 32.50 m
Displacement: 24,500 tons
Hull material: Sandwich structure, made of Nomex composite carbon fibers

Notes: Purchased at AmericaOne in 1997, then at the Seattle Challenge Team in 2000. After being bought by Bill Koch, it took part in the Jubilee 2001. It was displayed with the *America³* at the Museum of Fine Arts in Boston, along with Bill Koch's art collections.

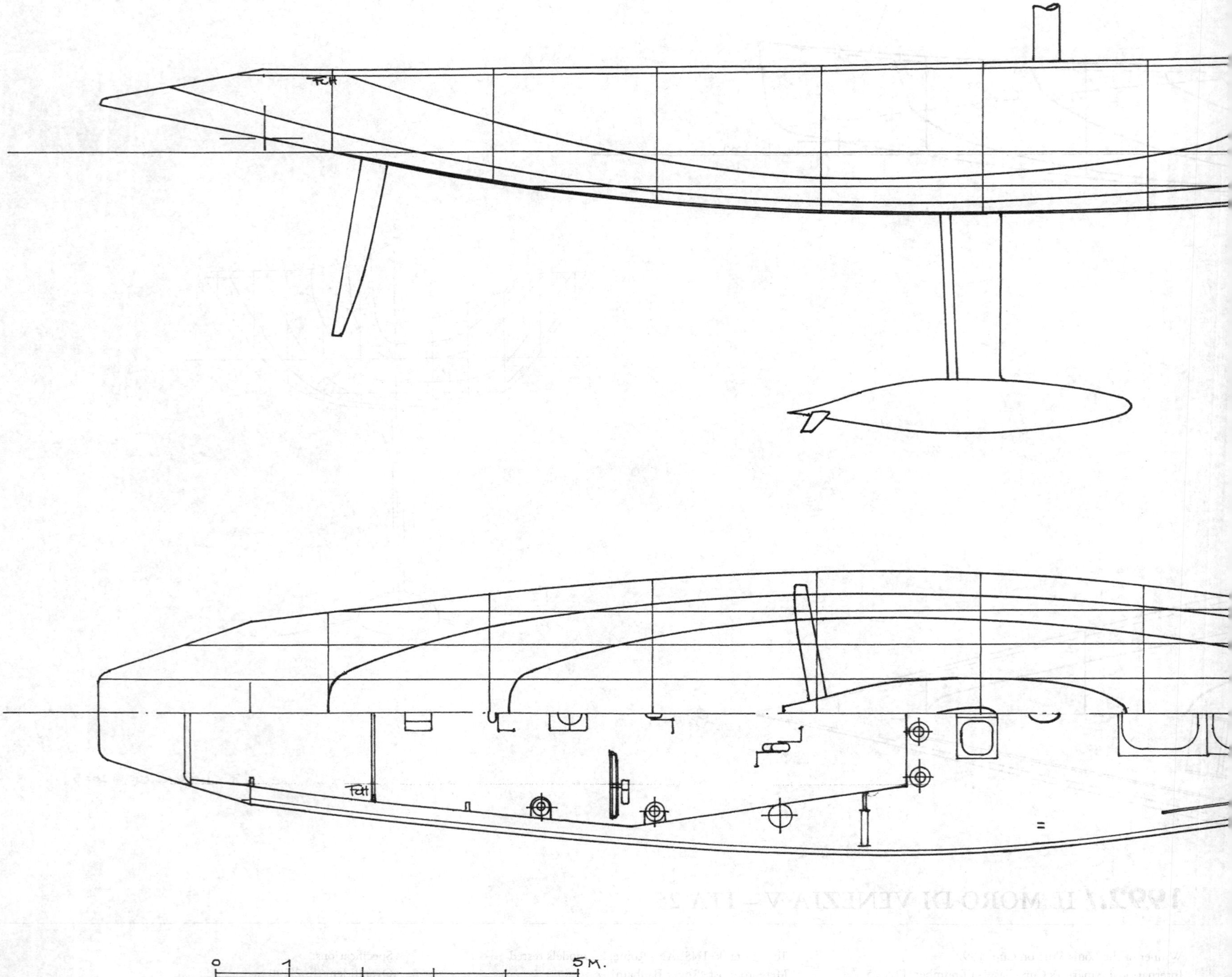

FCH
FCH
0
1
5 M.

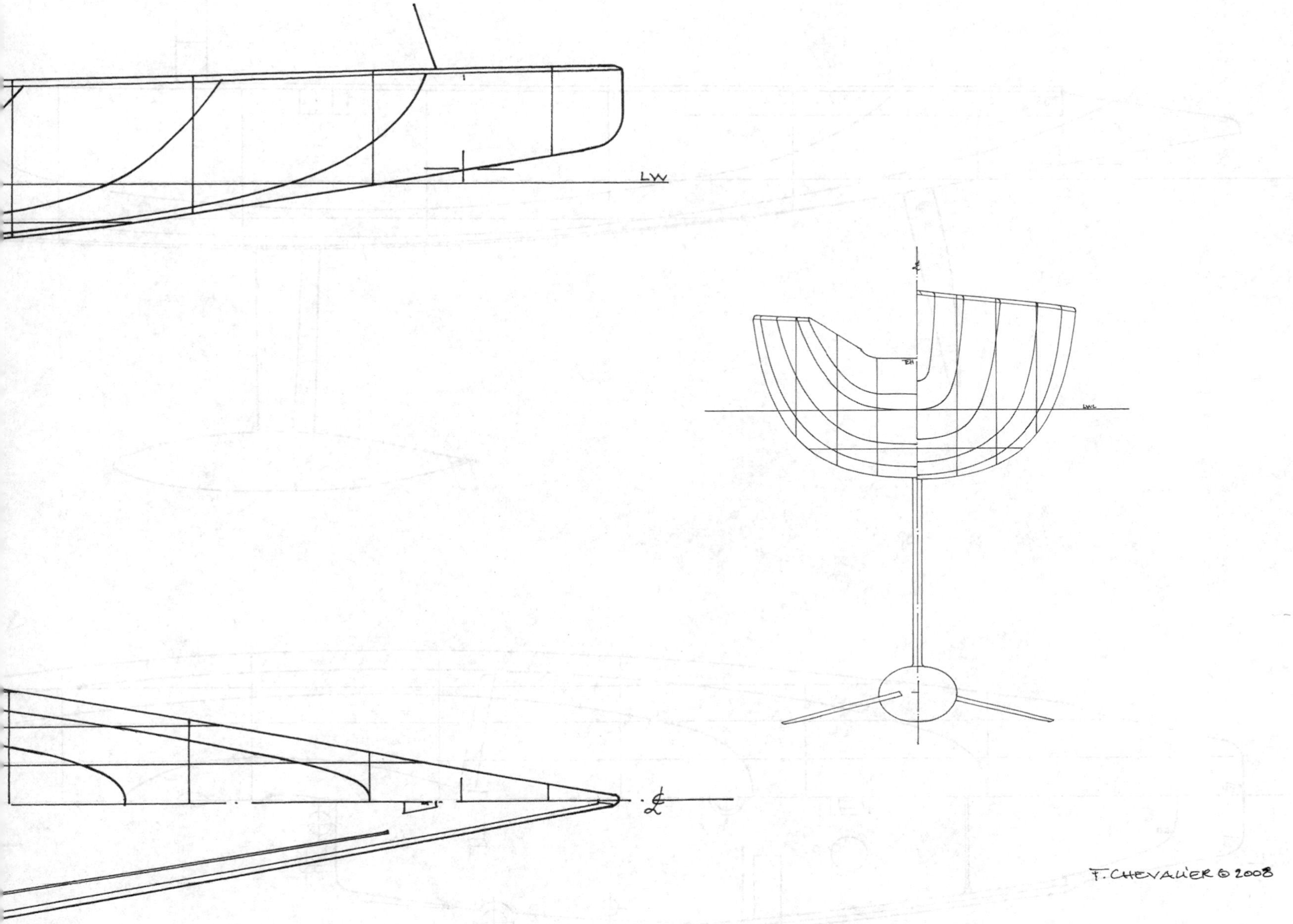

1995./ BLACK MAGIC – NZL 32

Winner of the Louis Vuitton Cup, 1995, and of the 29th America's Cup challenge in 1995
IACC, sail number: NZL 32
New Zealand
Yacht club: Royal New Zealand Yacht Squadron

Owner: Team New Zealand Syndicate, directed by Peter Blake
Sponsors: Toyota NZ, TVNZ, Loto, Enza, Lion Nathan (Steinlager)

Builder: McMullen & Wing yard, Auckland, New Zealand
Master sailmaker: Tom Schnackenberg, Team New Zealand, North Sails NZ

Architects: Doug Peterson and Laurie Davidson
Coordinator: Tom Schnackenberg
New Zealand Design Team: David Egan, Peter Jackson, Maury Leyland, David Alan-Williams

Aero- and Hydrodynamics: Richard Karn
Structure: Wayne Smith, Mike Drumond, Chris Mitchell & Neil Wilkinson
Towing tank: Great Britain
Wind tunnel testing: Prof. Peter Jackson

Launch: September 1993

Skipper: Russell Coutts
Tactician: Brad Butterworth
Navigator: Tom Schnackenberg
Crew: 16 + 1

Specifications:
Overall length: 24.24 m
Waterline length: 18.04 m
Bow: 4.05 m
Draft: 4 m
Sail surface area: 330 m^2
Spinnaker: 425 m^2
Mast height: 32.50 m
Displacement: 24,700 tons.
Hull material: Sandwich structure, made of Nomex composite carbon fibers

Notes: It was the training sailboat for Team New Zealand in 2000, then participated in the Jubilee 2001. Loaned to the French challenge team, it served for some time as a windbreaker for *FRA 46* and *FRA 69*. Upon returning to Auckland in July of 2002, it became the property of the New Zealand National Maritime Museum.

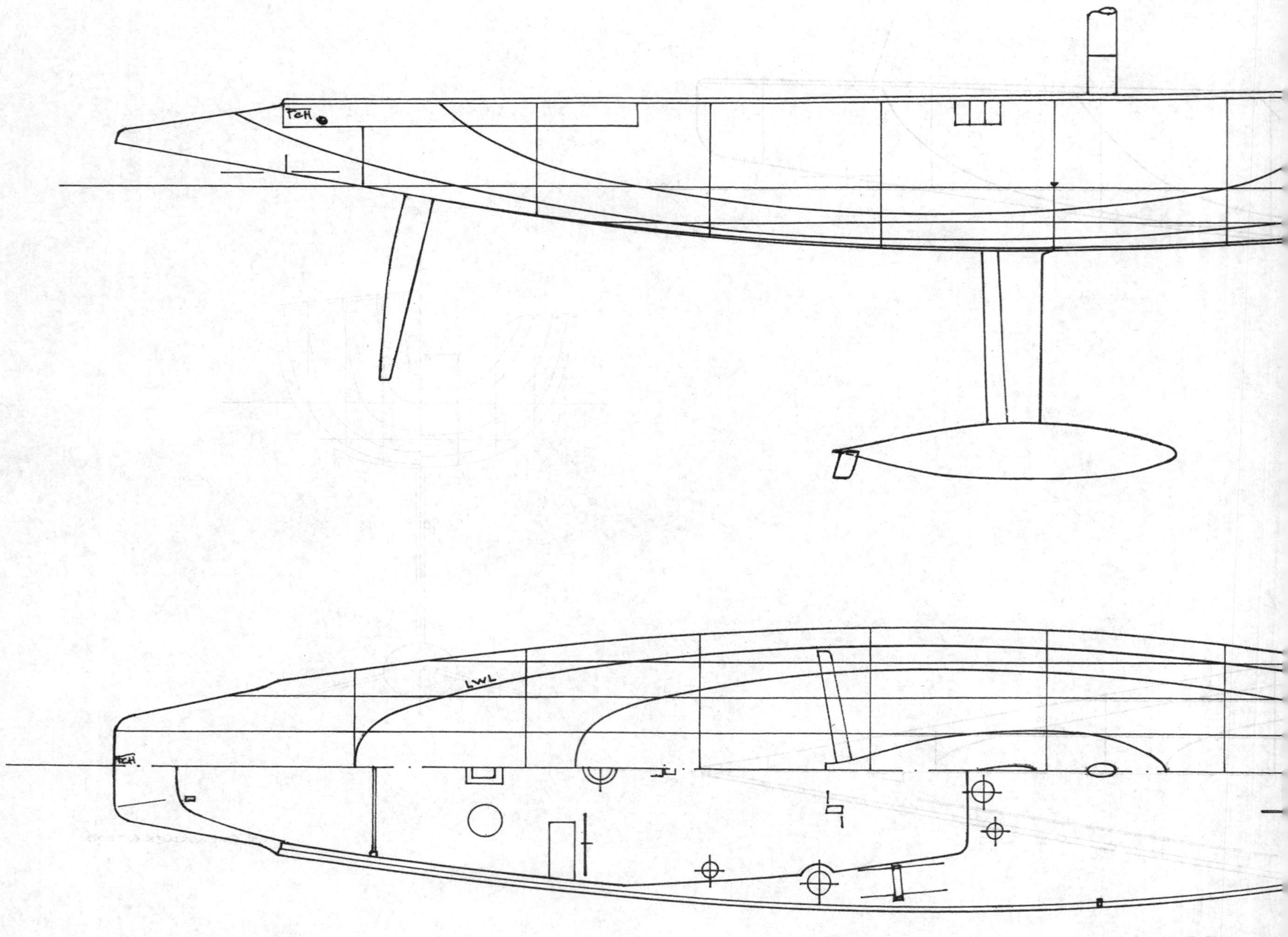
PCH
LWL
PCH

0
1
5M.

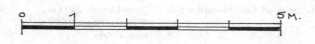

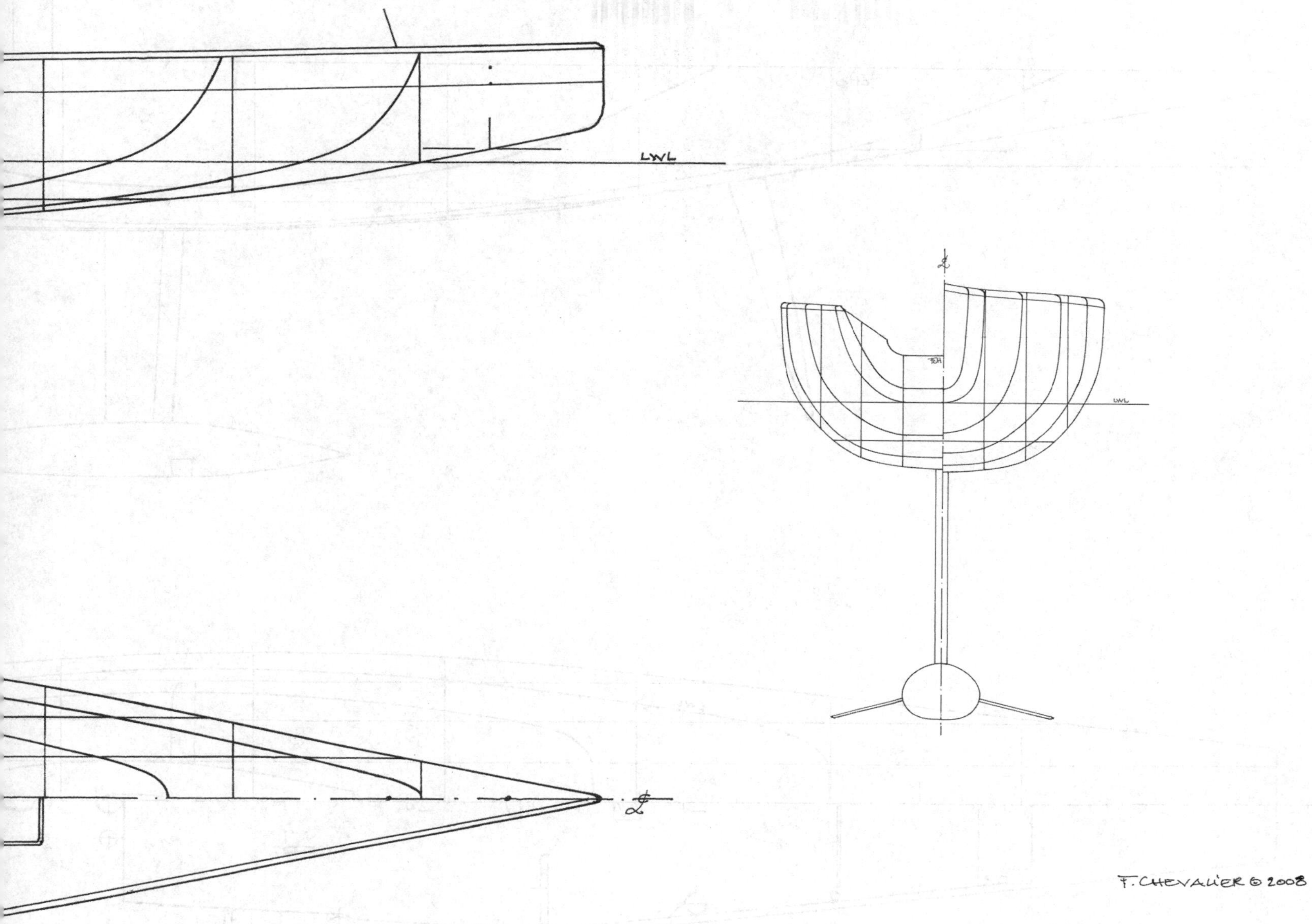

2000./ LUNA ROSSA – ITA 45

Winner of the Louis Vuitton Cup, 2000
IACC, sail number: ITA 45
Italy

Yacht club: Yacht Club Punta Ala
Commodore: Bruno Calandriello
Owner: Prada Challenge, presided over by Patrizio Bertelli
Director of Operations: Laurent Esquier

Builder: Prada
Spars and rigging: Southern Spars
Architect: German Frers, Doug Peterson, David Egan
Design team: German Frers, Jr., Miguel Costa, Claudio Maletto, Andrea Avaldi
Towing tank: INSEAN, Rome
Sail-loft: Guido Cavalazzi, sails North Sails Italia

Launch: May 5, 1999 at Punta Ala, delivery at Auckland, September 18

Skipper: Francesco de Angelis
Tactician: Torben Grael
Navigators: Matteo Plazzi, Dario Malgarise
Crew: 16 + 1
Training boat helmsman: Rod Davis

Specifications:
Overall length: 23.95 m
Waterline length: 18.30 m
Bow: 3.94 m
Draft: 4 m
Sail surface area: 326 m^2
Spinnaker: 425 m^2
Mast height: 32.50 m
Displacement: 24,600 tons
Hull material: Sandwich structure, made of Nomex composite carbon fibers

Notes: It participated in the Jubilee 2001, then served as a sail-training boat in 2002 and 2003 for Prada Challenge. In September 2005, it was exhibited in Rome at the Piazza del Popolo.

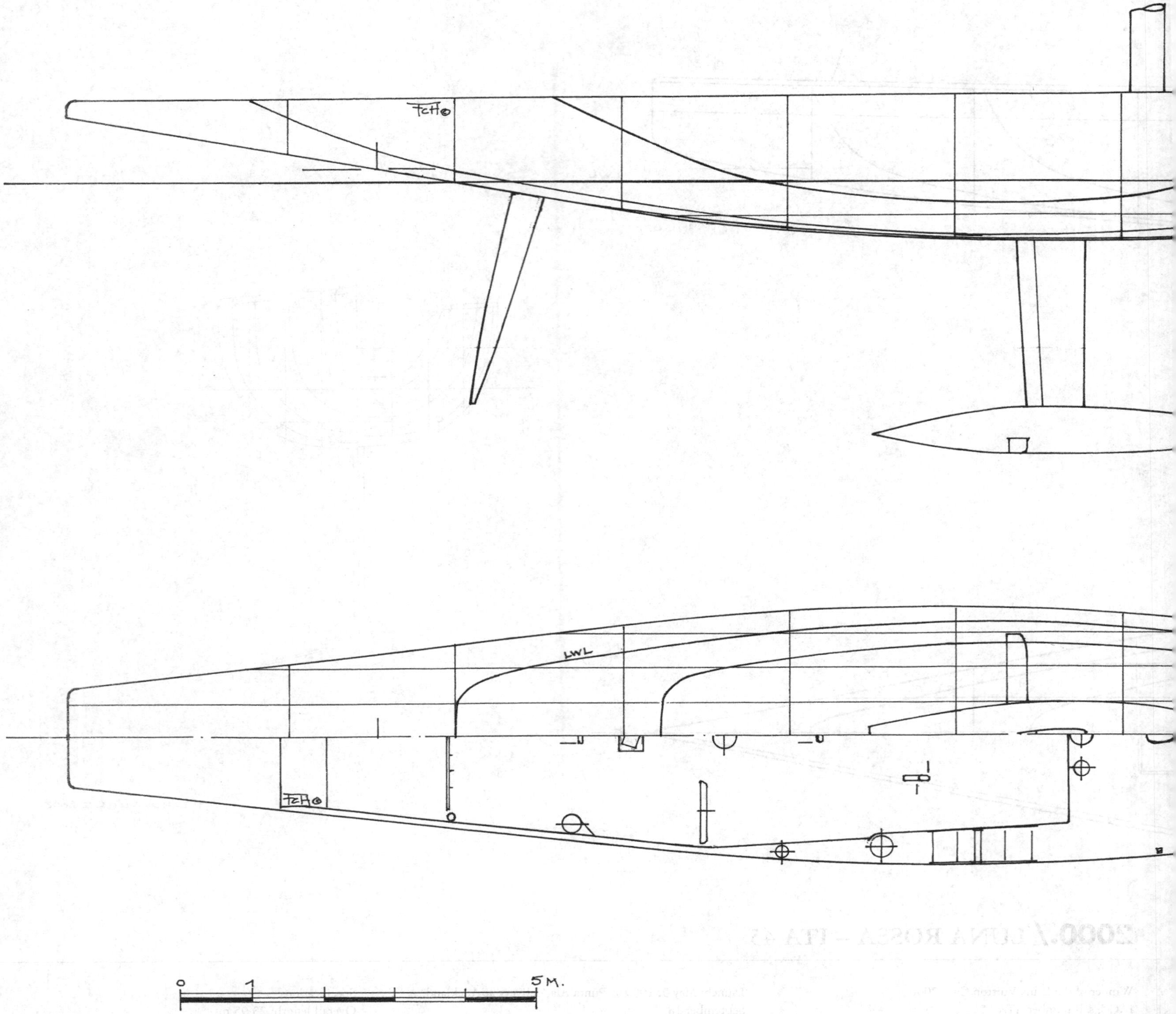
FcH©
LWL
FcH©
0
1
5M.

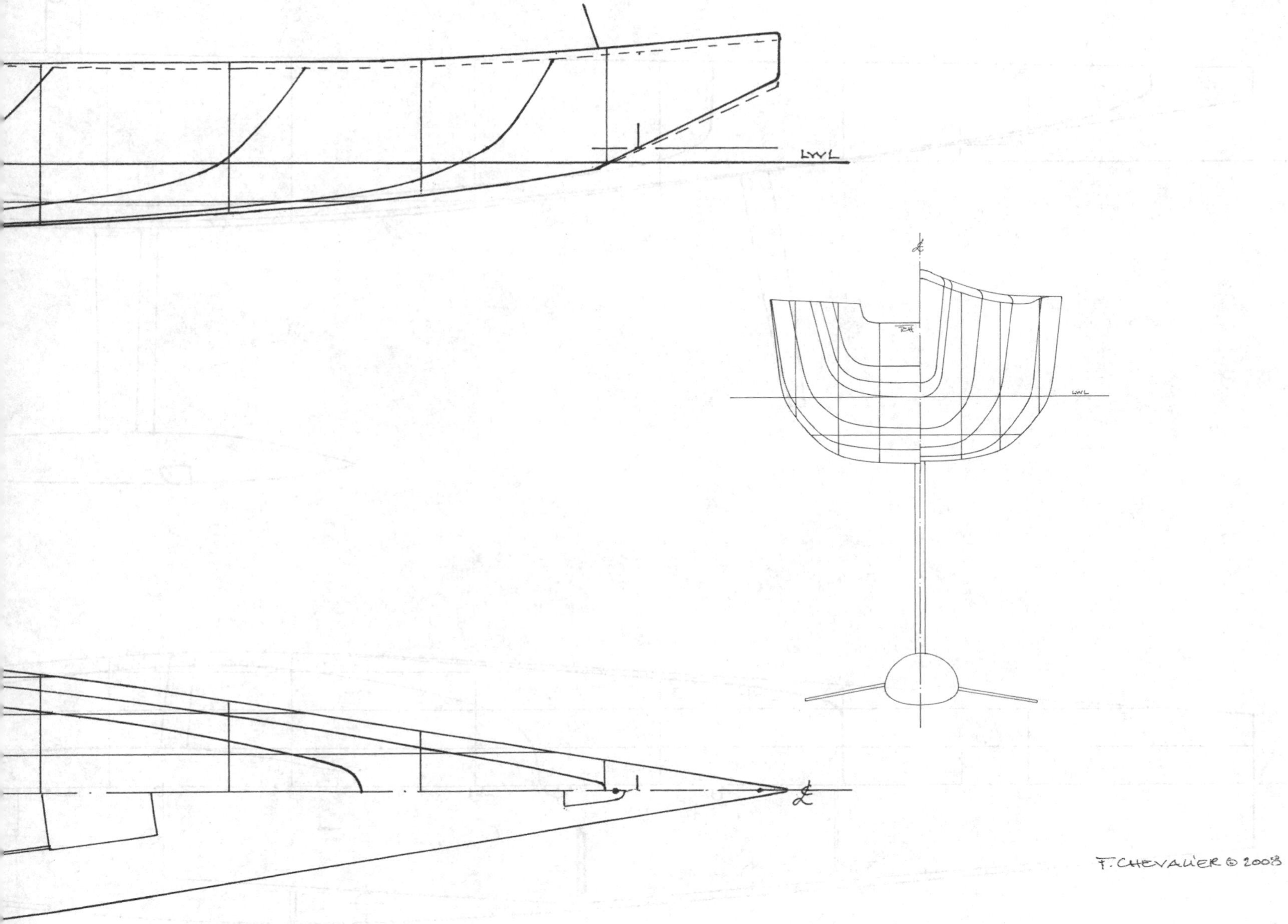

2003./ ALINGHI – SUI 64

Winner of the Louis Vuitton Cup, 2003, and
of the 31st America's Cup challenge in 2003
IACC, sail number: SUI 64
Switzerland
Yacht club: Société Nautique de Genève

Owner: Syndicate Alinghi, directed by Ernesto Bertarelli
Sponsors: UBS, Infonet, Audemars Piguet, Riri
Builder: Decision SA, Fenil-sur-Corsier, division of Vaud, Suisse
Bertrand Cardis
Sails: North Sails
Architects: Rolf Vrolijk
Coordinator: Grant Simmer

Design Team: Manuel Ruiz de Elvira, Dirk Kramers,
Mike Schreiber
Research: Ecole Polytechnique Fédérale de Lausanne (EPFL)

Launch: November 20, 2001

Skipper: Russell Coutts
Tactician: Brad Butterworth
Navigator: Ernesto Bertarelli
Crew: 16 + 1

Specifications:
Overall length: 26.24 m
Waterline length: 18.65 m
Bow: 3.75 m
Draft: 4 m
Sail surface area: 330 m²
Spinnaker: 425 m²
Mast height: 32.50 m
Displacement: 24,800 tons.
Hull material: Sandwich structure, made of Nomex composite carbon fibers

Notes: Property of the Alinghi Syndicate in Valencia, Spain.

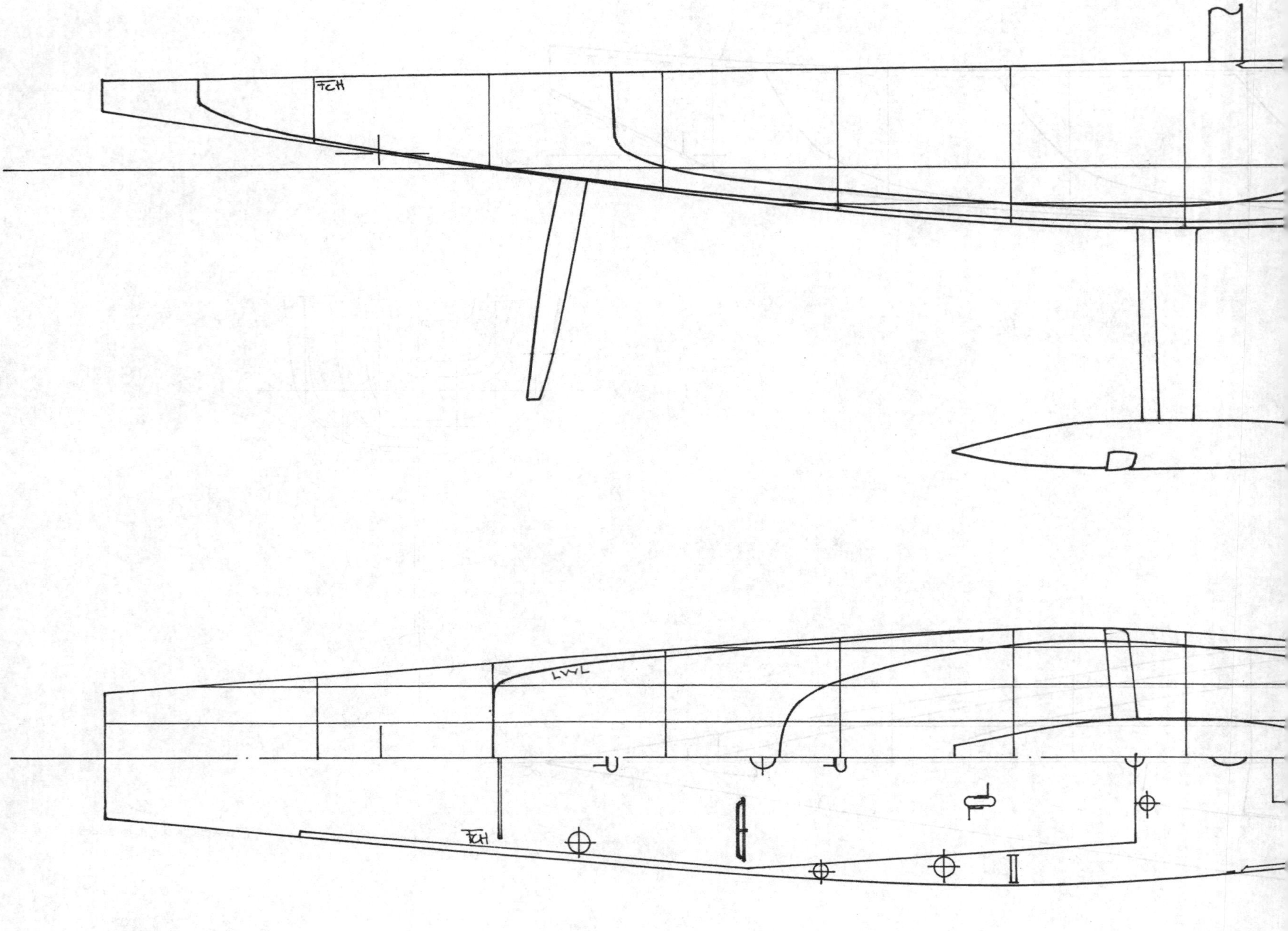
FCH
LWL
FCH
0
1
5 M.

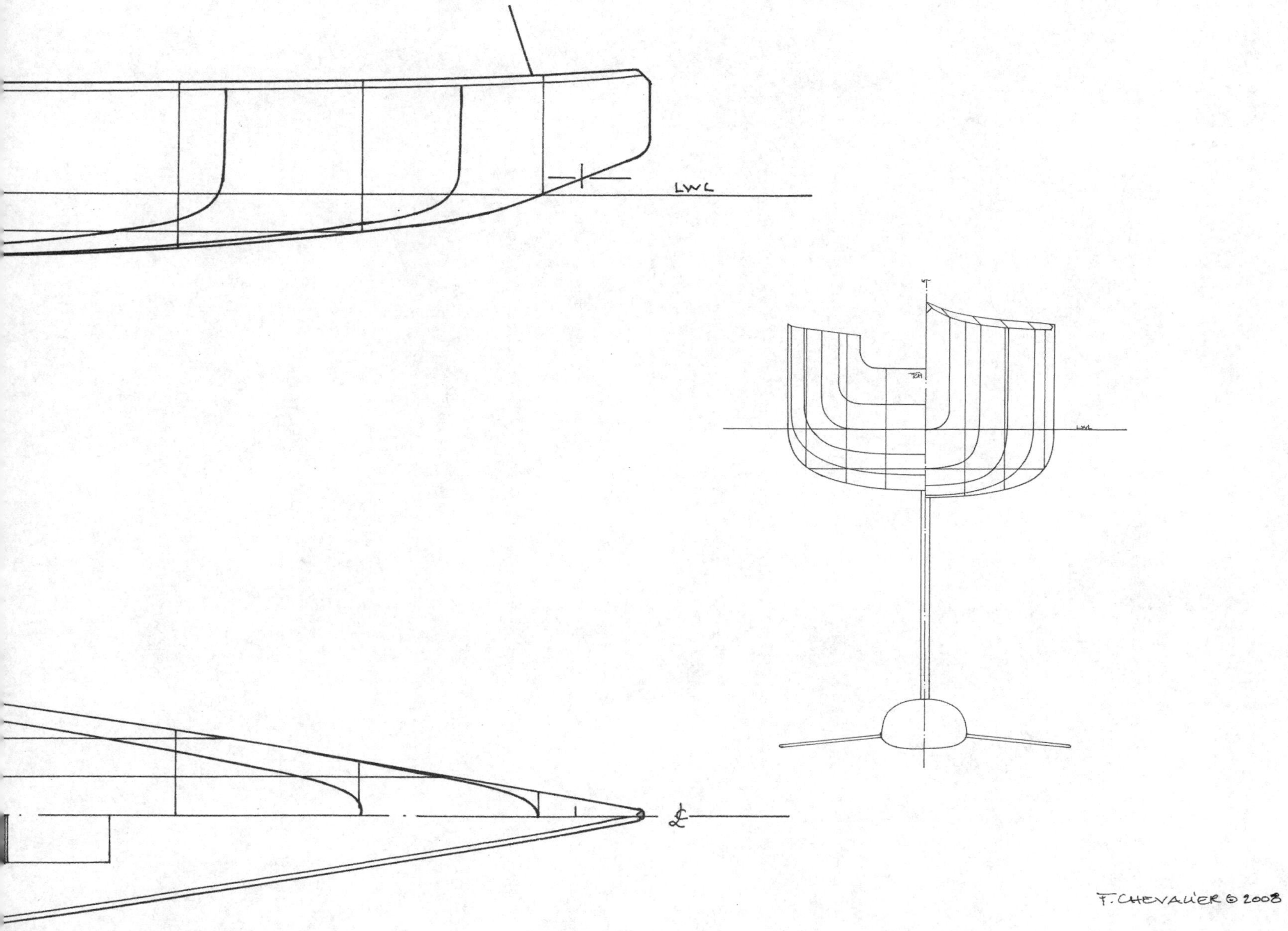

2007./ TEAM NEW ZEALAND – NZL 92

Winner of the Louis Vuitton Cup, 2007
IACC, sail number: NZL 92
New Zealand
Yacht club: Royal New Zealand Yacht Squadron

Owner: Emirates Team New Zealand Syndicate, directed by Grant Dalton
Sponsors: Fly Emirates, Toyota NZ, Estrella Damm

Builder: Cookson's Boatyard, Auckland, New Zealand
Master sailmaker: Burns Fallow, Robert Hook, North Sails NZ
Architects: Andy Claughton, Marcelino Botin, Clay Oliver
Emirates New Zealand Design Team: Nick Holroyd, Nick Hutchins

Structure: Giovanni Belgrano, Andrew Kensington, Darryl Senn, Adam Greenwood
Wind tunnel testing: University of Auckland

Christening: June 24, 2006, by prime minister Helen Clark in Auckland

Skipper: Dean Barker
Tactician: Terry Hutchinson
Navigator: Kevin Hall
Crew: 17 + 1

Specifications:
Overall length: 24.75 m
Waterline length: 18.25 m
Bow: 3.37m
Draft: 4.10 m
Sail surface: 320 m²
Spinnaker: 425 m²
Mast height: 32.50 m
Displacement: 24 tons
Hull material: Sandwich structure, made of Nomex composite carbon fibers

Notes: Property of Emirates Team New Zealand Syndicate

EXTRAS

CHALLENGERS
CHARTS
CIRCUITS
DRAWINGS
STATISTICS
BIOGRAPHIES
PHOTO COLLAGE
GLOSSARY
ACKNOWLEDGMENTS
BIBLIOGRAPHY
INDEX

1./ NEWPORT, RHODE ISLAND 1983

Conditions for the Louis Vuitton Cup, 1983

The Challenger of Record: Royal Sydney Yacht Squadron
Sailboats: International 12-Meter Class, where the waterline is longer than 44 feet, or 13.41 meters.
Formula:

$$\frac{L + 2d + \sqrt{S} - F}{2.37} = 12 \text{ meter}$$

L = rated length in meters, taken 18 cm above the waterline
d = difference between chain and girth
S = area of sail, including mainsail and front triangle
F = correction for the freeboard

The displacement varies with the length (L), as well as the draft. Eleven crew members on board each boat.

Qualifiers: Three round robins, A, B, and C; semifinals, where each team meets three times; and finals, for four victories.
Each challenger must build and equip its boats in its own country; the crew must be of the challenger's nationality.

Challengers: 7
Nations: 5

Australia II
Australia
Royal Perth Yacht Club
Alan Bond
Skipper: **John Bertrand**
*Australia II KA 6**
Architect: Ben Lexcen
Builder: Steve E. Ward & Co., Cottesloe

Victory 83 Challenge
England
Royal Burnham Yaht Club
Peter de Savary
Skippers: **Harold Cudmore, Phil Crebbin, Lawrie Smith, Rodney Pattison**
Victory 82 K 21
*Victory 83 K 22**
Architects: Ian Howlett, Ed Dubois
Builders: Fairey Allday Marine, William A. Souter & Son

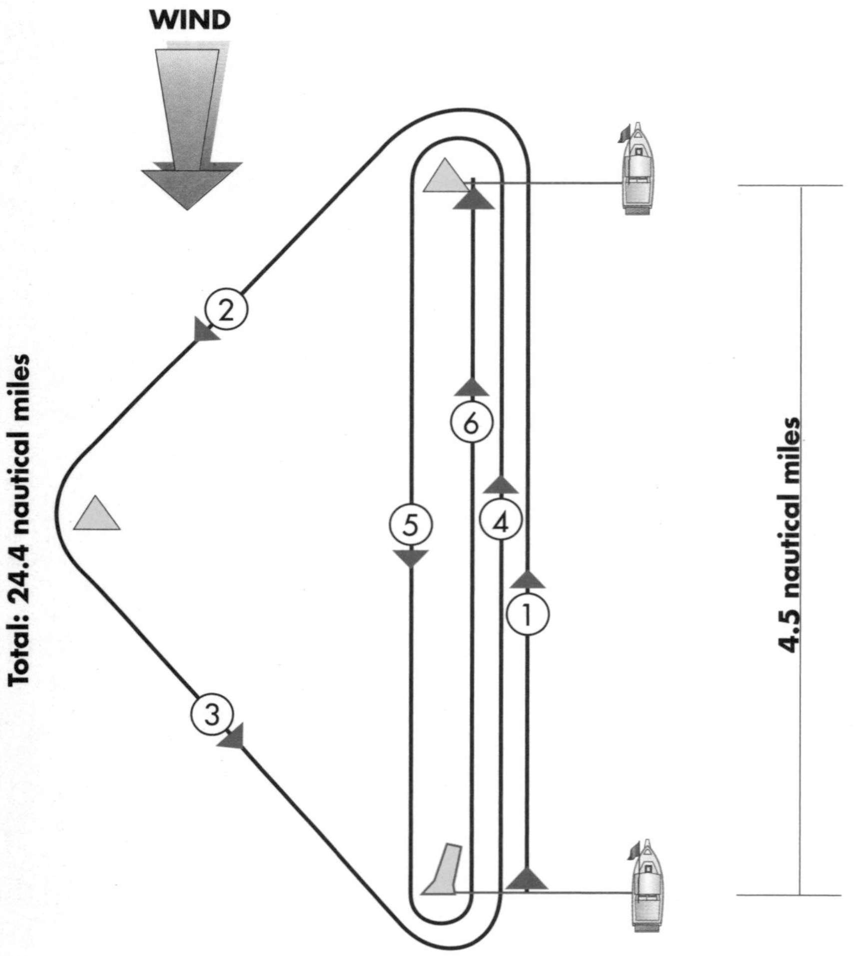

Newport Circuit 1983
Drawing by François Chevalier

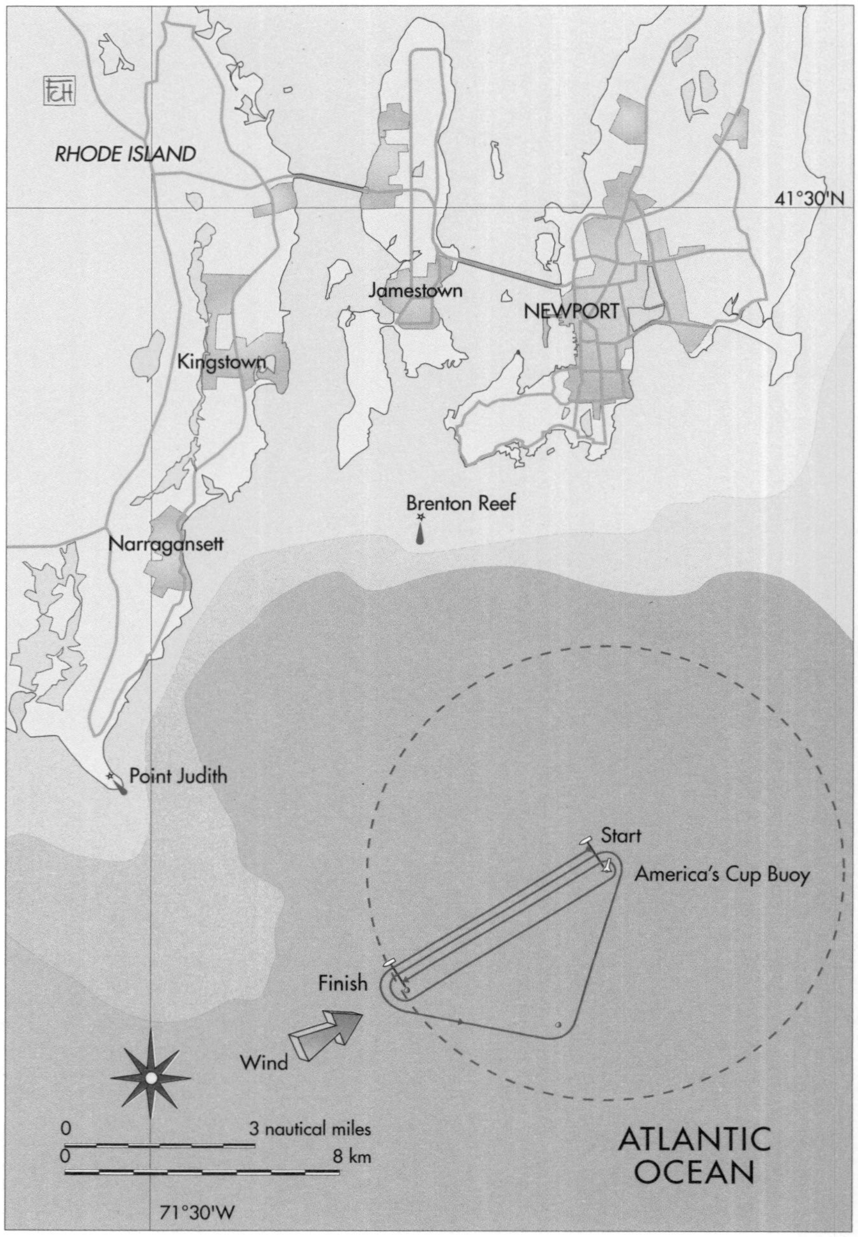

Newport Chart 1983
Drawing by François Chevalier

Sfida Italiana America Cup 1983
Italy
Costa Smeralda Yacht Club
Gian Franco Alberini
Skipper: **Lino Ricci**
*Azzurra I 4**
Architect: Andrea Vallicelli
Builder: Marco Corbau, Yachts Officine Pesaro

Canadian America's Cup Challenge
Canada
Secret Cove Yacht Club
Don Keary
Skipper: **Terry McLaughlin**
*Canada 1 KC 1**
Architect: Bruce Kirby
Builder: Fred MacConnell Marine

Challenge 12
Australia
Royal Victoria Yacht Club, Melbourne
Rod Ledgar
Skipper: **John Savage**
*Challenge 12 KA 10**
Architect: Ben Lexcen
Builder: Steve E. Ward & Co., Cottesloe

Défi Français pour la Coupe de l'America
France
Yacht Club de France
Henri de Maublanc
Skipper: **Bruno Troublé**
*France 3 F 3**
Architects: Johan Valentijn, Jacques Fauroux
Builder: Chantiers Dufour

Advance
Australia
Royal Sydney Yacht Squadron
Syd Fischer
Skipper: **Iain Murray**
*Advance KA 7**
Architect: Alan Payne
Builder: Aquacraft Yacht

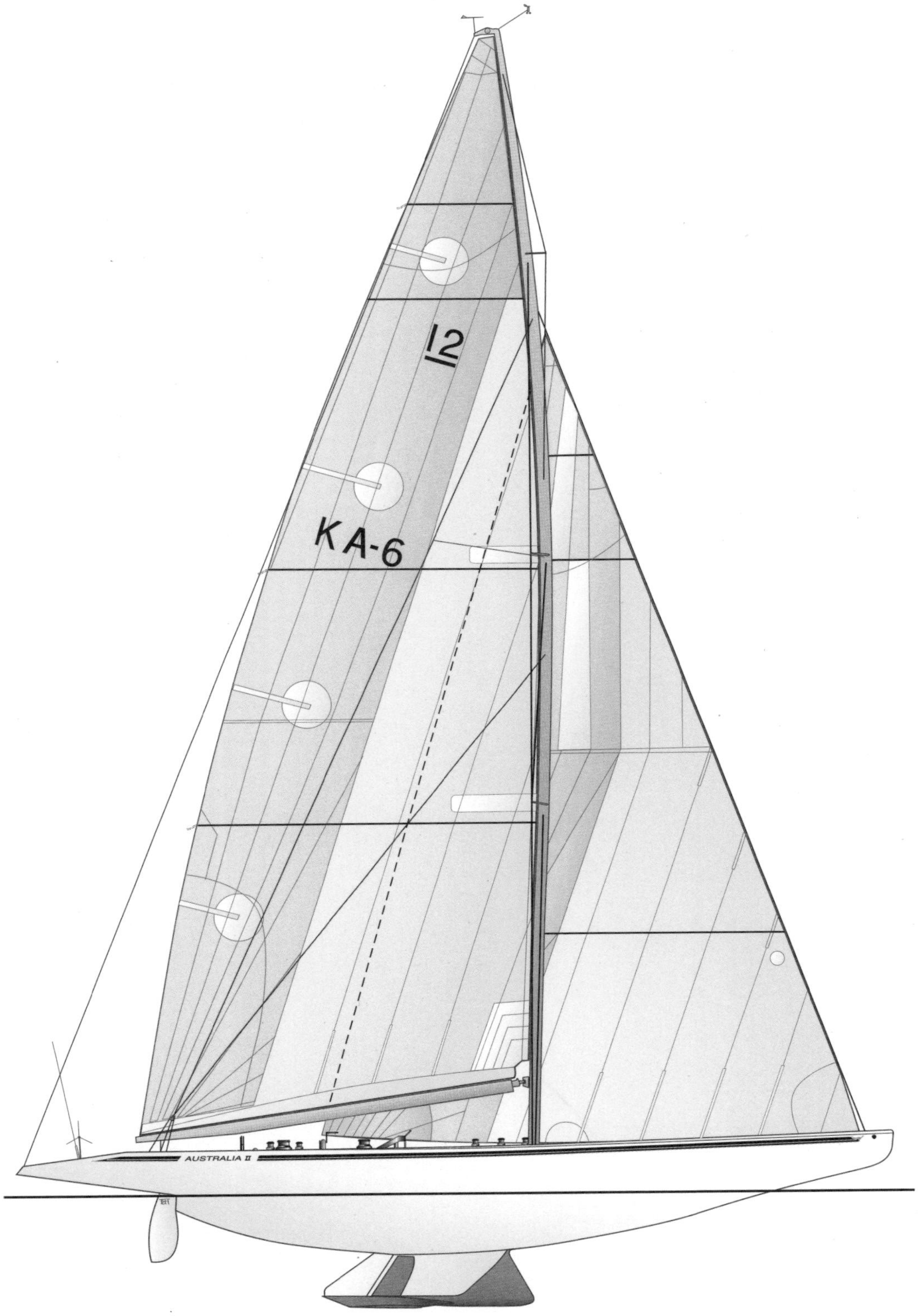

Australia II
Drawing by François Chevalier

1./ LOUIS VUITTON CUP RESULTS 1983

Round Robin A – June 18 to June 28

	Australia II	Challenge 12	Victory 83	Azzurra	Canada 1	France 3	Advance	Wins
Australia II	/	•	••	••	••	••	••	11
Challenge 12	•	/	•	••	••	••	••	10
Victory 83		•	/	•	••	••	••	8
Azzurra			•	/	•	•	••	5
Canada 1				•	/	•	••	4
France 3				•	•	/	••	4
Advance							/	0

Results count at 20%

Round Robin B – July 2 to July 14

	Australia II	Challenge 12	Victory 83	Azzurra	Canada 1	France 3	Advance	Wins
Australia II	/	••	•	•	••	••	••	10
Challenge 12		/	•	••	•	••	••	8
Victory 83	•	•	/	•	•	••	•	7
Azzurra	•		•	/	•	••	••	7
Canada 1		•	•	•	/	••	•	6
France 3						/	••	2
Advance			•		•		/	2

Results count at 40%

Round Robin C – July 12 to August 6

	Australia II	Challenge 12	Victory 83	Azzurra	Canada 1	France 3	Advance	Wins	Points
Australia II	/	•••	•••	••	•••	••	••	15	19.88
Challenge 12		/	••	•••	••	••	••	11	13.44
Victory 83		•	/	•	•••	••	••	9	12.20
Azzurra	•		••	/	•	••	••	8	11.72
Canada 1		•		••	/	••	••	7	10.80
France 3						/	•	1	2.12
Advance							/	0	0.80

Semifinals – August 11 to August 24

	Australia II	Victory 83	Azzurra	Canada 1
Australia II	/	••	•••	•••
Victory 83	•	/	••	•••
Azzurra		•	/	•••
Canada 1				/

Finals – August 28 to September 8

	1	2	3	4	5	
Australia II		•	•	•	•	4
Victory 83	•					1

2./ FREMANTLE, AUSTRALIA 1987

Conditions for the Louis Vuitton Cup, 1987

Challenger of Record: Yacht Club Costa Smeralda
Sailboats: International 12-Meter Class
Qualifiers: Three round robins; semifinals, where two groups meet for four victories; finals, for four victories.
The challengers may, if they wish, change boats between the first and second round robin, but lose their acquired points by doing so.

Challengers: 15
Nations: 6

Sail America
United States
San Diego Yacht Club
Malin Burnham
Skipper: **Dennis Conner**
Stars & Stripes '83 US 53 (formerly *Spirit of America*)
Stars & Stripes '85 US 54
Stars & Stripes '86 US 56
*Stars & Stripes '87 US 55**
Architects: Britton Chance, Bruce Nelson, Dave Pedrick
Builders: Robert E. Derecktor, Inc.

RNZ America's Cup Challenge
New Zealand
Royal New Zealand Yacht Squadron
H. Michael Fay
Skipper: **Chris Dickson**
New Zealand KZ 3
New Zealand KZ 5
*New Zealand KZ 7**
Architects: Bruce Farr, Ron Holland, Laurie Davidson
Builders: McMullen & Wing, Marten Marine

Saint Francis Golden Gate Challenge
United States
Saint Francis Yacht Club
Robert D. Scott
Skipper: **Tom Blackaller**
USA I US 49
*USA II US 61**
Architects: Gary Mull, Alberto Calderon
Builders: Robert E. Derecktor, Inc.

Challenge Kiss France
France
Société des Régates Rochelaises, Société Nautique de Sète
Marc Pajot, Serge Crasnianski
Skipper: **Marc Pajot**
*French Kiss F 7**
Architect: Philippe Briand
Builder: Alubat, Pouvreau

America II Challenge
United States
New York Yacht Club
Thomas F. Ehman Jr.
Skipper: **John Kolius**
America II US 42
America II US 44
*America II US 46**
Architects: Sparkman & Stephens (Bill Langan)
Builders: Williams & Manchester

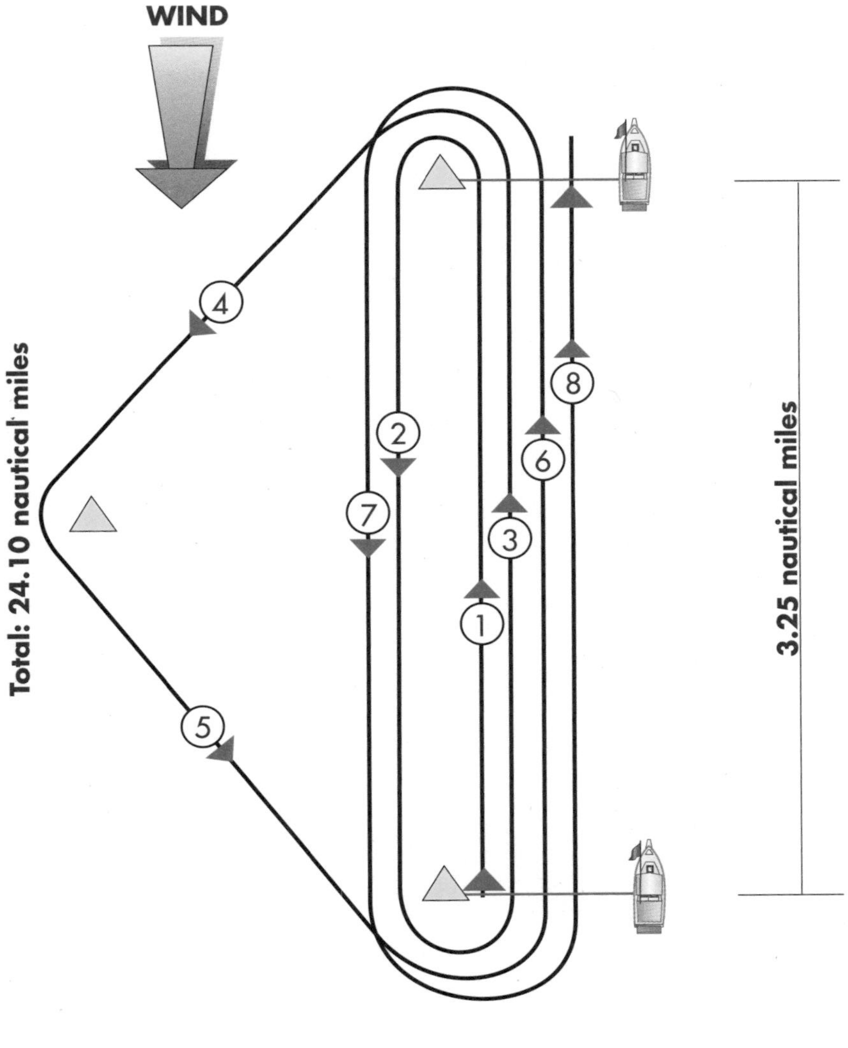

Fremantle Circuit 1987
Drawing by François Chevalier

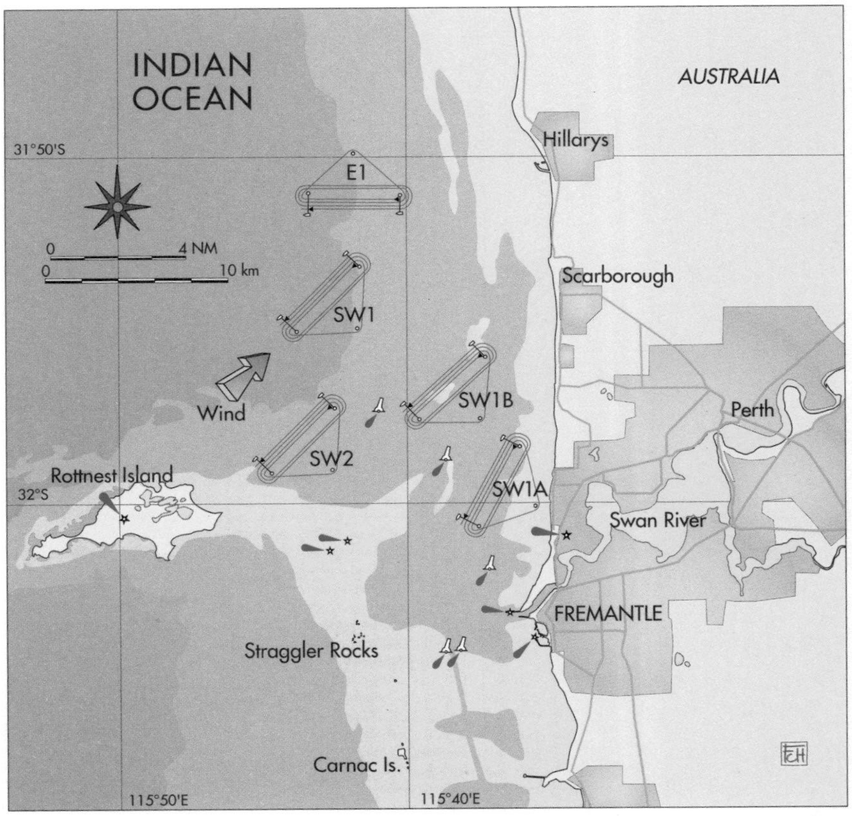

Fremantle Chart 1987
Drawing by François Chevalier

British America's Cup Challenge 1987
Great Britain
Royal Thames Yacht Club
Graham Walker
Skipper: **Harold Cudmore**
*White Crusader I K 23**
White Crusader II ("Hippo") K 25
Architects: Ian Howlett, David Hollom
Builder: Cougar Marine

Consorzio Italia
Italy
Yacht Club Italiano
Angelo Monassi
Skipper: **Aldo Migliaccio**
Italia I I 7
*Italia II I 9**
Architects: Giorgetti & Magrini
Builder: Baglietto, Leghe Leggere Yachts

Heart of America Challenge
United States
Chicago Yacht Club
Eugene M. Kinney
Skipper: **Harry C. Buddy Melges, Jr.**
*Heart of America US 51**
Architects: Graham & Schlageter
Builder: Merrifield Roberts Inc.

Canadian America's Cup Challenge
Canada
Secret Cove Yacht Club
Marvin V. MacDill
Skipper: **Terry Neilson**
*Canada II KC 2**
True North KC 87
Architects: Bruce Kirby, Steve Killing
Builders: Canadian Marine

Eagle Challenge
United States
Newport Harbour Yacht Club
James P. Warmington
Skipper: **Rod Davis**
*Eagle US 60**
Architect: Johan Valentijn
Builder: Williams & Manchester

Consorzio Azzurra
Italy
Yacht Club Costa Smeralda
Riccardo Bonadeo
Skipper: **Mauro Pelaschier**
*Azzurra III I 10**
Azzurra IV I 11
Architect: Andrea Vallicelli
Builder: SAI Ambrosini

Challenge France
France
Société Nautique de Marseille
Yves Pajot
Skipper: **Yves Pajot**
*Challenge France F 8**
Architect: Daniel Andrieu
Builder: Aerospatiale

Courageous Syndicate
United States
Yale Corinthian Yacht Club
Leonard Greene
Skipper: **David Vietor**
*Courageous IV US 26**
Architects: Sparkman & Stephens, L. Greene
Builder: Minnefords

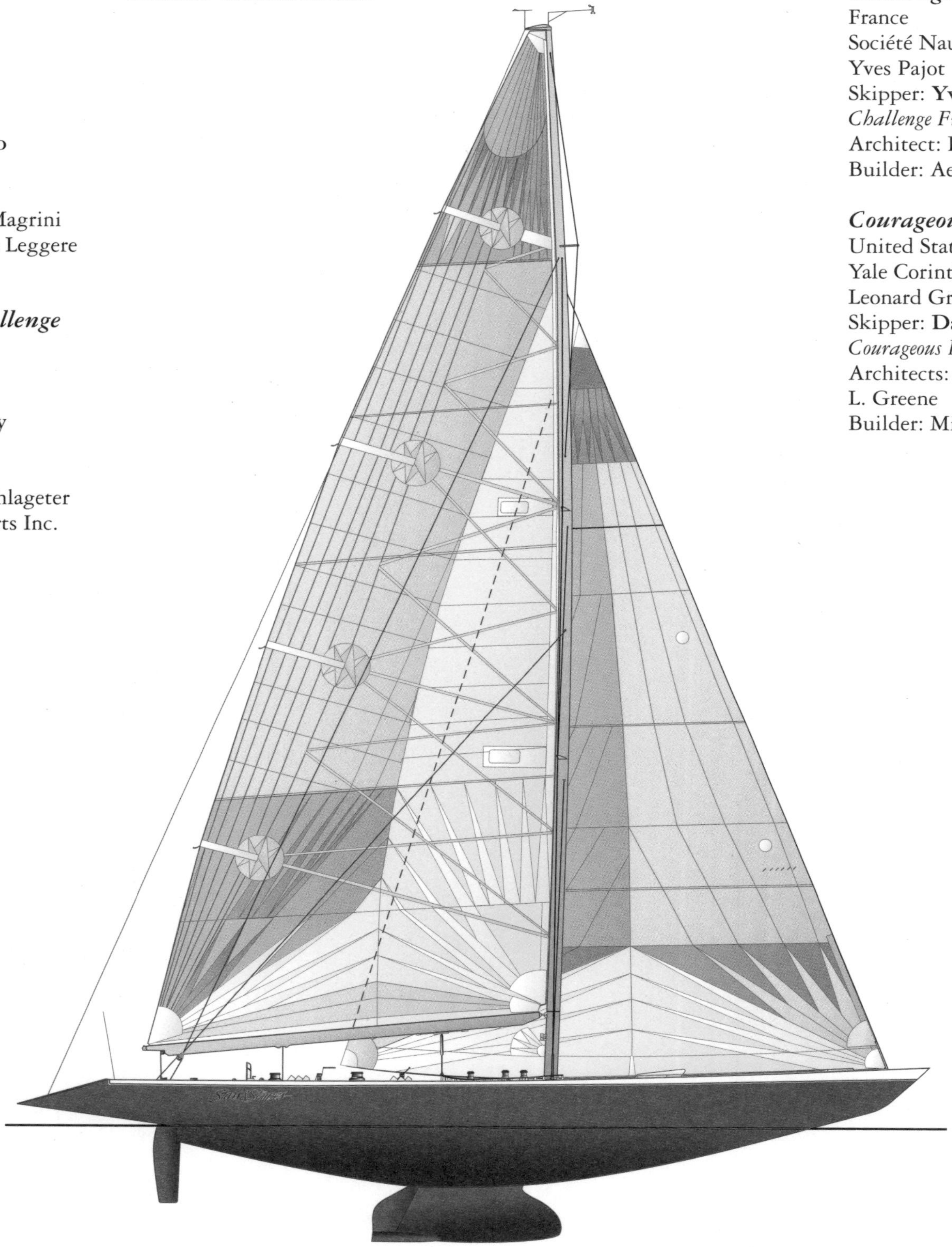

Stars & Stripes '87 US 55
Drawing by François Chevalier

2./ LOUIS VUITTON CUP RESULTS 1986–1987

Round Robin 1 – October 5 to 20, 1986

	America II	New Zealand	Stars & Stripes	USA	White Crusader	Italia	Canada II	French Kiss	Eagle	Heart of America	Challenge France	Azzurra	Courageous IV	Wins
America II	/		•	•	•	•	•	•	•	•	•	•	•	11
New Zealand	•	/		•	•	•	•	•	•	•	•	•	•	11
Stars & Stripes		•	/	•	•	•	•	•	•	•	•	•	•	11
USA				/		•	•	•	•	•	•	•	•	8
White Crusader				•	/		•	•	•	•	•	•	•	8
Italia					•	/	•		•	•	•	•	•	7
Canada II							/	•	•	•	•	•	•	6
French Kiss					•			/	•	•		•	•	5
Eagle									/	•	•	•	•	4
Heart of America										/	•	•	•	3
Challenge France								•			/	•		2
Azzurra												/	•	1
Courageous IV											•		/	1

- One point per win

Round Robin 2 – November 2 to 19, 1986

	New Zealand	America II	French Kiss	Stars & Stripes	USA	White Crusader	Canada II	Italia	Eagle	Heart of America	Azzurra	Challenge France	Courageous IV	Wins
New Zealand	/	•	•	•	•	•	•	•	•	•	•	•		11
America II		/		•	•	•	•	•	•	•	•	•		9
French Kiss			/		•	•	•	•	•	•	•	•		8
Stars & Stripes				/		•	•	•	•	•	•	•		7
USA				•	/	•	•	•		•	•	•		7
White Crusader				•		/	•	•	•	•	•	•		7
Canada II				•			/		•	•	•	•		5
Italia						•	/		•	•		•		4
Eagle					•				/	•	•	•		4
Heart of America						•				/		•		2
Azzurra							•				/	•		2
Challenge France												/		0
Courageous IV													/	0

- Five points per win

Round Robin 3 – December 2 to 19, 1986

	New Zealand	Stars & Stripes	USA	French Kiss	America II	White Crusader	Italia	Heart of America	Canada II	Eagle	Azzurra	Challenge France	Courageous IV	Wins	Points
New Zealand	/	•	•	•	•	•	•	•	•	•	•	•		11	198
Stars & Stripes		/		•	•	•	•	•	•	•	•	•		9	154
USA		•	/		•	•		•	•	•	•	•		8	139
French Kiss				/	•	•		•	•	•	•	•		7	129
America II					/	•	•		•	•	•	•		6	128
White Crusader						/	•	•	•	•	•	•		6	115
Italia			•	•			/	•		•	•	•		6	99
Heart of America		•			•			/	•	•	•	•		6	85
Canada II							•		/	•	•	•		4	79
Eagle										/	•	•		2	48
Azzurra											/	•		1	23
Challenge France												/		0	2
Courageous IV													/	0	1

- Twelve points per win

Semifinals – December 20 to January 4, 1987

	Stars & Stripes	USA
Stars & Stripes	/	••••
USA		/

	New Zealand	French Kiss
New Zealand	/	••••
French Kiss		/

Finals – January 1 to 5, 1987

	1	2	3	4	5	
Stars & Stripes	•	•		•	•	4
New Zealand			•			1

3./ SAN DIEGO, CALIFORNIA 1992

Conditions for the Louis Vuitton Cup, 1992

Challenger of Record: Royal Perth Yacht Club
Sailboats: International America's Cup Class (IACC)

Formula:

$$\frac{L + 1.25\sqrt{S} - 98\sqrt[3]{D}}{0.388} = 42 \text{ meter}$$

L = rated length in meters
S = rated sail area in square meters
D = displacement in cubic meters
L and S are limited by the attached formulas

The maximum beam is to 5.5 meters.
The maximum draft is 4 meters.
The displacement must be between 16 and 25 tons.
Carbon construction, hull and mast.
Maximum height of mast is 32.5 meters.
16 crew members and one guest.
Qualifiers: Three round robins; semifinals, in which each team meets three times; and finals, for five wins.
The number of boats built by the challenger is open.
An onboard judge, or umpire, accompanies the competitors and gives his verdicts on site. On request by the competitor, the judge can hand out a penalty turn that must be carried out before the finish line.
Advertising on the mainsail or the spinnaker is legal.

Challengers: 8
Nations: 7

Il Moro di Venezia
Italy
Compagnia della Vela
Raul Gardini
Skipper: **Paul Cayard**
Il Moro di Venezia ITA 1
Il Moro di Venezia II ITA 7
Il Moro di Venezia III ITA 15
Il Moro di Venezia IV ITA 16
*Il Moro di Venezia V ITA 25**
Architect: German Frers
Builder: Tencara Shipyard, Porto Marghera

New Zealand Challenge
New Zealand
Mercury Bay Boating Club
Sir Michael Fay
Skipper: **Rod Davis**
New Zealand NZL 10
New Zealand NZL 12
New Zealand, NZL 14
*New Zealand, NZL 20**
Architects: Bruce Farr, Russell Bowler
Builders: Marten Marine, Cookson Boats

Le Défi Français
France
Yacht Club de France-Sète
Yvon Jacob
Skipper: **Marc Pajot**
Ville de Paris FRA 1
Ville de Paris FRA 8
*Ville de Paris FRA 27**
Architect: Philippe Briand
Builders: MAG France, VMG, Pinta

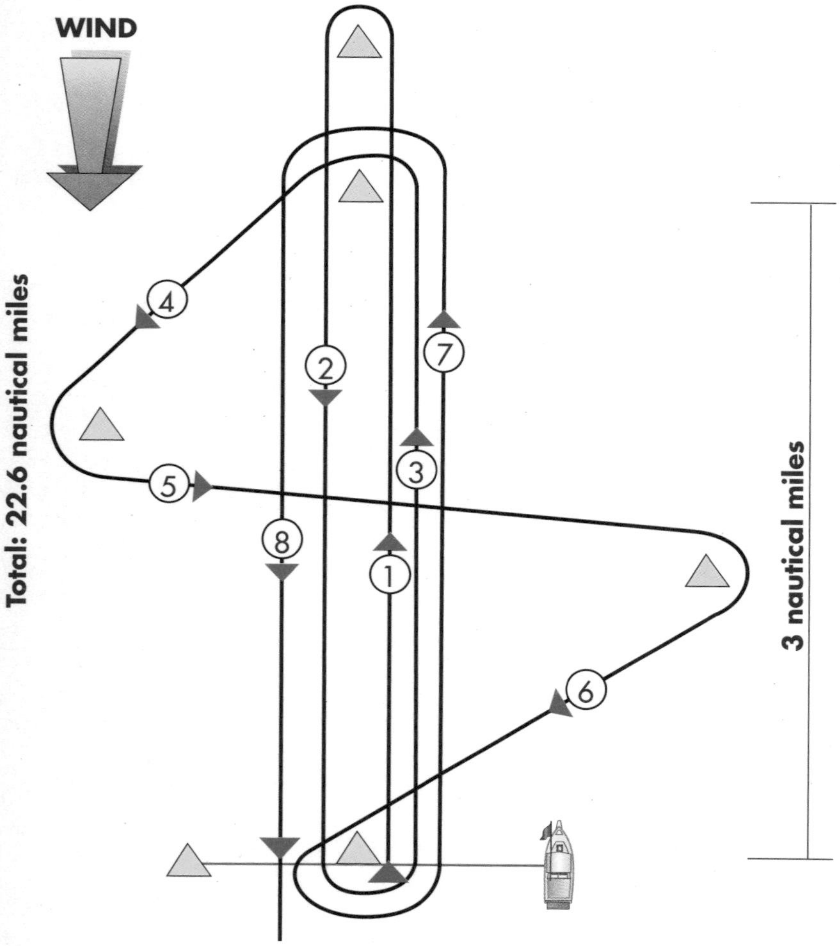

San Diego Circuit 1992
Drawing by François Chevalier

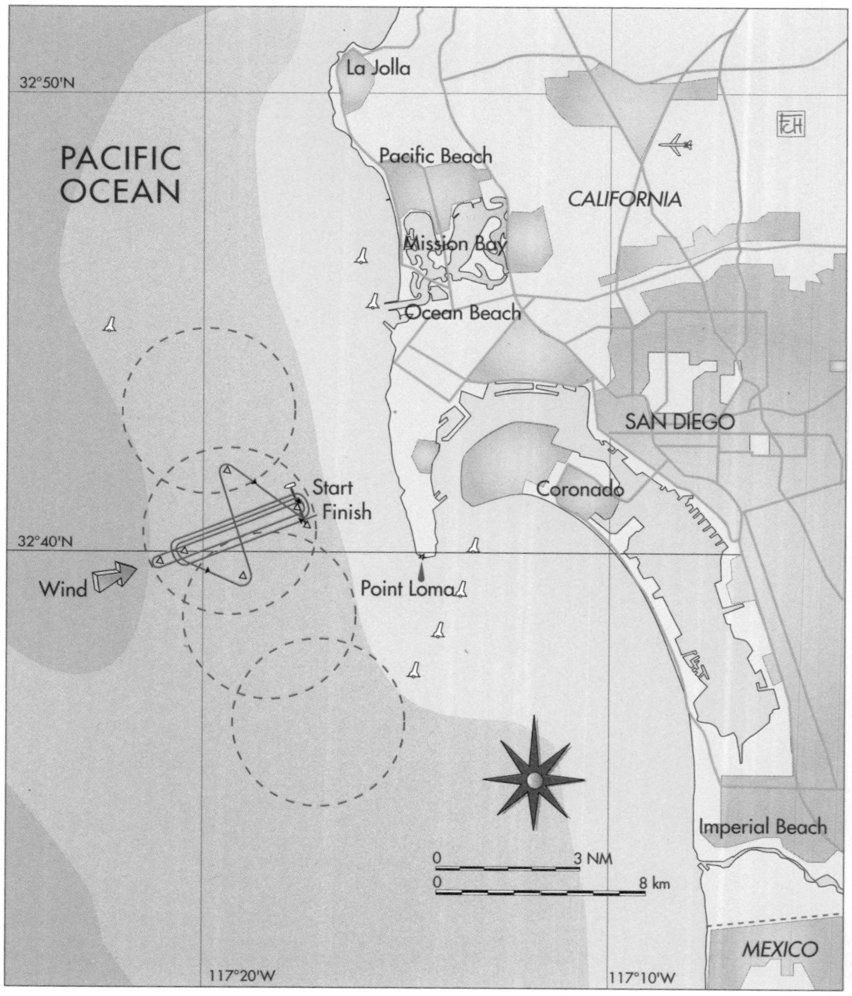

San Diego Chart 1992
Drawing by François Chevalier

Nippon Challenge for the America's Cup
Japan
Nippon Ocean Racing Club
Tatsumitsu Yamasaki
Skipper: **Chris Dickson**
Nippon JPN 3
Nippon JPN 6
*Nippon JPN 26**
Architect: Ichiro Yokoyama
Builder: Yahama Motor Co.

Desafío Español Copa America
Spain
Monte Real Club de Yates de Bayona
Eduardo Serra Rexach
Skipper: **Pedro Campos**
España 92 ESP 5
*España 92 ESP 22**
Architects: Diego Colon, Inigo Echenique
Builder: Astilleros Espanoles, Cadiz

Spirit of Australia
Australia
Darling Harbour Yacht Club
Iain Murray
Skipper: **Peter Gilmour**
*Spirit of Australia AUS 21**
Architect: Iain Murray
Builder: John McConaghy

Swedish America's Cup Challenge
Sweden
Stenungsbaden Yacht Club
Tomas Wallin
Skipper: **Gunnar Krantz**
*Tre Kronor SWE 19**
Architects: Peter Norlin, Lars Bergstrom
Builder: Killian Bushe

Challenge Australia
Australia
Royal Sydney Yacht Squadron
Syd Fischer
Skipper: **Phil Thompson**
*Challenge Australia AUS 17**
Architect: Peter Van Oossanen
Builder: John McConaghy

Il Moro di Venezia V ITA 25
Drawing by François Chevalier

3./ LOUIS VUITTON CUP RESULTS 1992

Round Robin 1 – January 25 to February 2

	Nippon	New Zealand	Ville de Paris	Il Moro di Venezia	Spirit of Australia	España 92	Tre Kronor	Challenge Australia	Wins
Nippon	/		•	•	•	•	•	•	6
New Zealand	•	/	•		•	•	•	•	6
Ville de Paris			/	•	•	•	•	•	5
Il Moro di Venezia		•		/	•	•	•	•	5
Spirit of Australia					/	•	•	•	3
España 92						/	•	•	2
Tre Kronor							/	•	1
Challenge Australia								/	0

- One point per win

Round Robin 2 – February 15 to 23

	New Zealand	Il Moro di Venezia	Nippon	Ville de Paris	España 92	Spirit of Australia	Tre Kronor	Challenge Australia	Wins
New Zealand	/	•	•	•	•	•	•	•	7
Il Moro di Venezia		/	•	•	•	•	•	•	6
Nippon			/	•	•	•	•	•	5
Ville de Paris				/	•	•	•	•	4
España 92					/	•	•	•	3
Spirit of Australia						/	•	•	2
Tre Kronor							/	•	1
Challenge Australia								/	0

- Four points per win

Round Robin 3 – March 7 to 15

	Nippon	New Zealand	Il Moro di Venezia	Ville de Paris	España 92	Spirit of Australia	Tre Kronor	Challenge Australia	Wins	Points
Nippon	/	•	•	•	•	•	•	•	7	82
New Zealand		/	•		•	•	•	•	5	74
Il Moro di Venezia			/	•	•	•	•	•	5	69
Ville de Paris	•			/	•	•	•	•	5	61
España 92					/		•	•	2	30
Spirit of Australia					•	/	•		2	27
Tre Kronor							/	•	1	13
Challenge Australia						•		/	1	8

- Eight points per win

Semifinals – March 29 to April 7

	New Zealand	Il Moro di Venezia	Ville de Paris	Nippon	New Zealand	Il Moro di Venezia	Ville de Paris	Nippon	New Zealand	Il Moro di Venezia	Ville de Paris	Nippon	Wins
New Zealand	/	•		•	/		•	•	/	•	•	•	7
Il Moro di Venezia		/	•	•	•	/		•		/	•		5
	•		/	•		•	/				/	•	4
Nippon				/			•	/		•		/	2

- One point per win

Finals – April 19 to 30

	1	2	3	4	5	6	7	8	9	
Il Moro di Venezia		•				•	•	•	•	5
New Zealand	•		•	can						3

- can: *Cancelled*

4./ SAN DIEGO, CALIFORNIA 1995

Conditions for the Louis Vuitton Cup, 1995

Challenger of Record: Yacht Club de France-Sète
A Challenger of Record Committee (CORC) is created by the challengers.
Sailboats: International America's Cup Class (IACC)
Qualifiers: Four round robins; semifinals in which each team races four times; and the finals, for best of five.
The number of sailboats built by the challenger is limited to two, and the number of sails to 45.
The challengers can change boats between two series of regattas.
The members of a challenge must have been residents of the challenge's country for at least two years.
On April 9, 1995, "unveiling day," the finalists of the Louis Vuitton Cup and the Citizen's Cup—the selection regattas for the American defense—will raise the tarpaulins that cover their boats, so the public can see their designs.
Advertising is permitted on the mainsail and the spinnaker.
Louis Vuitton provides publicity for the Citizen Cup and the America's Cup.

Challengers: 7
Nations: 5

Team New Zealand
New Zealand
Royal New Zealand Yacht Squadron
Peter Blake
Skipper: **Russell Coutts**
*Black Magic NZL 32**
*Black Magic NZL 38**
Architects: Doug Peterson, Laurie Davidson
Builder: McMullen & Wing

oneAustralia
Australia
Southern Cross Yacht Club
John Bertrand
Skipper: **John Bertrand**
*oneAustralia AUS 31**
*oneAustralia AUS 35**
Architects: Iain Murray, John Reichel
Builder: John McConaghy

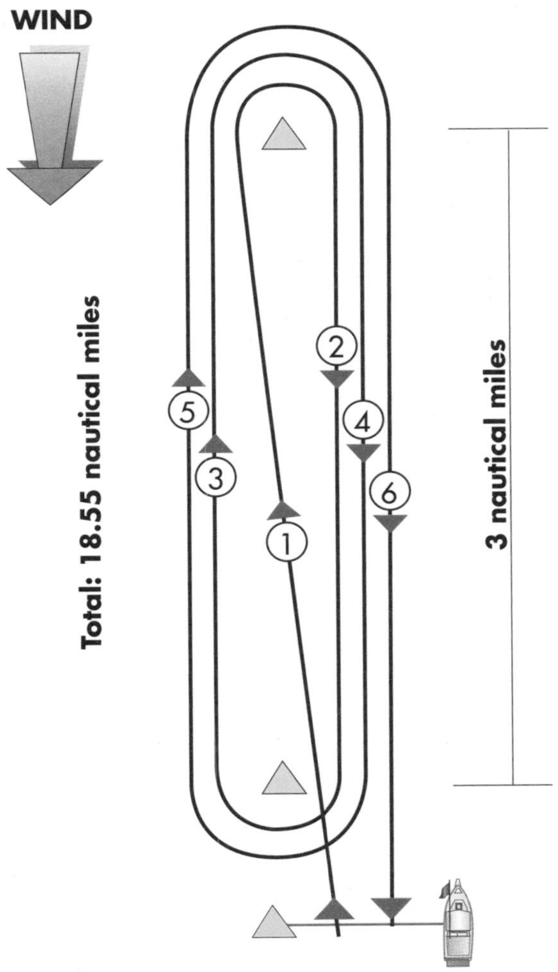

San Diego Circuit 1995
Drawing by François Chevalier

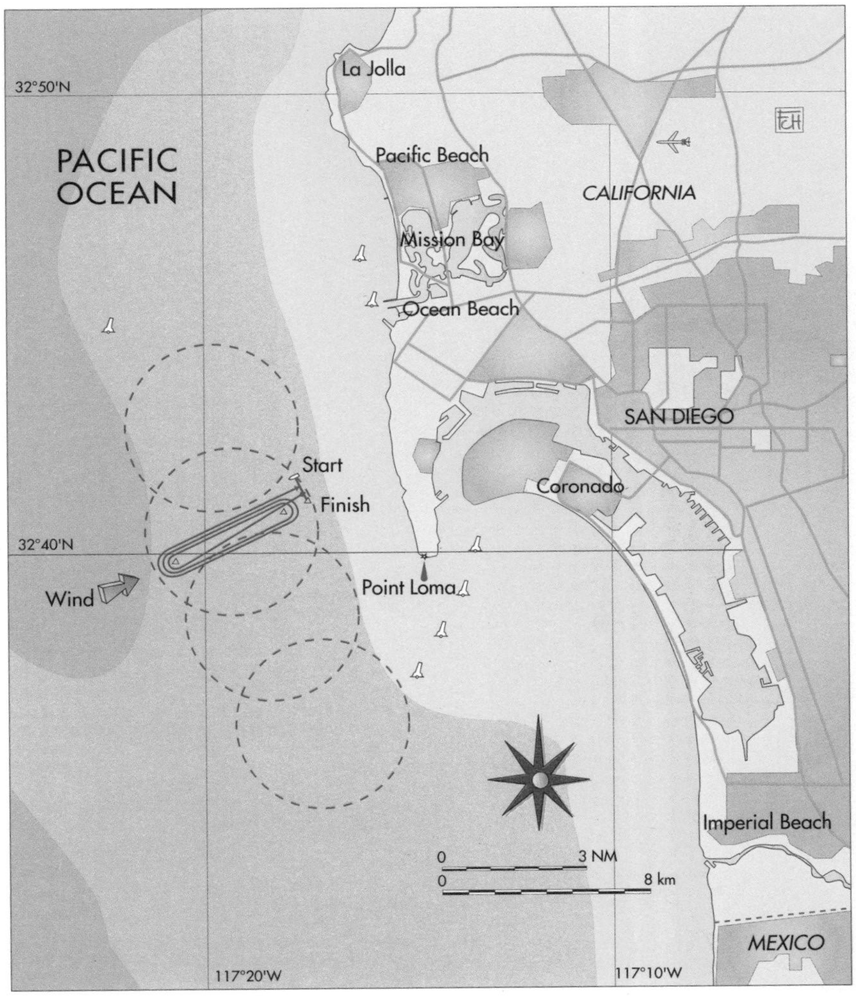

San Diego Chart 1995
Drawing by François Chevalier

Tag Heuer Challenge
New Zealand
Tutukaka South Pacific Yacht Club
Chris Dickson
Skipper: **Chris Dickson**
*Tag Heuer NZL 39**
Architect: Bruce Farr
Builder: Cookson Boats

Nippon Challenge
Japan
Nippon Yacht Club
Tatsumitsu Yamasaki
Skipper: **Makoto Namba**
*Nippon JPN 30**
*Nippon JPN 41**
Architect: Ichiro Yokoyama
Builder: Yahama

France America '95
France
Yacht Club de France-Sète
François Giraudet
Skipper: **Marc Pajot**
*France 2 FRA 33**
*France 3 FRA 37**
Architect: Philippe Briand
Builder: Jeanneau, MAG France

Copa America '95 Desafío Español
Spain
Monte Real Club de Yates de Bayona
Real Club Nautica de Valencia
Miguel Aguilo
Skipper: **Pedro Campos**
*Rioja de España 92 ESP 42**
Architect: Joaquin Coello
Builder: Rodman Polyships, Vigo

Australian Challenge
Australia
Australian Yacht Club
Syd Fischer
Skipper: **Neville Wittey**
*Sydney 95 AUS 29**
Architects: Iain Murray, John Reichel
Builder: John McConaghy

Black Magic NZL 32
Drawing by François Chevalier

4./ LOUIS VUITTON CUP RESULTS 1995

Round Robin 1 – January 4 to 20

	Black Magic	NZL 39	Nippon	oneAustralia	Sydney 95	France II	Rioja de España	Wins
Black Magic	/	•	•	•	•	•	•	6
NZL 39		/	•	•	•	•	•	5
Nippon			/	•	•	•	•	4
oneAustralia				/	•	•	•	3
Sydney 95					/	•	•	2
France II						/	•	1
Rioja de España							/	0

- *One point per win*

Round Robin 2 – January 24 to February 7

	Black Magic	NZL 39	oneAustralia	Nippon	France III	Sydney 95	Rioja de España	Wins
Black Magic	/	•	•	•	•	•	•	6
NZL 39		/		•	•	•	•	4
oneAustralia		•	/		•	•	•	4
Nippon			•	/		•	•	3
France III				•	/	•	•	3
Sydney 95						/	•	1
Rioja de España							/	0

- *Two points per win*

Round Robin 3 – February 15 to 22

	Black Magic	oneAustralia	NZL 39	Nippon	France III	Sydney 95	Rioja de España	Wins
Black Magic	/	•	•	•	•	•	•	6
oneAustralia		/	•	•	•	•	•	5
NZL 39			/	•	•	•	•	4
Nippon				/		•	•	2
France III				•	/		•	2
Sydney 95					•	/		1
Rioja de España						•	/	1

- *Four points per win*

Round Robin 4 – March 2 to 8

	Black Magic	oneAustralia	NZL 39	Nippon	France III	Rioja de España	Sydney 95	Wins	Points
Black Magic	/		•	•	•	•	•	5	13
oneAustralia		/	•	•		•	•	4	53
NZL 39			/	•	•	•	•	4	25
Nippon				/	•	•		2	28
France III		•			/		•	2	65
Rioja de España					•	/	•	2	49
Sydney 95				•	•		/	2	14

- *Five point per win*

Semifinals – March 18 to 31

	Black Magic	oneAustralia	NZL 39	Nippon	Black Magic	oneAustralia	NZL 39	Nippon	Black Magic	oneAustralia	NZL 39	Nippon	Black Magic	oneAustralia	NZL 39	Nippon	Total
Black Magic	/	•	•	•	/	•	•	•	/	•	•	•	/	dns	dns	dns	9
oneAustralia		/		•		/	•	•		/	•	•	•	/	dns	•	7
NZL 39		•	/	•			/	•			/	•	•	dns	/	•	6
Nippon				/				/				/	•			/	1

- dns: *Did not start*

Finals – April 11 to 20

	1	2	3	4	5	6	
Black Magic	•	•	•		•	•	5
oneAustralia				•			1

5./ AUCKLAND, NEW ZEALAND 2000

Conditions for the Louis Vuitton Cup, 2000

The Challenger of Record, the New York Yacht Club, assembles a Challenger of Record Committee. Sailboats: International America's Cup Class (IACC). The numbers for the formula for the capacity have been modified so that the result is equal to 24, the approximate length of the boats in meters.

$$\frac{L + 1.25\sqrt{S} - 98\sqrt[3]{D}}{0.677} = 24 \text{ meter}$$

Qualifiers: Three round robins; semifinals, in which each team meets three times; and finals, for five wins. During the first round robin, the boats make one fewer circuits.

The number of boats built by each challenge is limited to two. The challengers can modify or change their boats between two round robins.
The members of a challenge must be residents for at least two years of the country they represent.
At the end of the Louis Vuitton Cup, "unveiling day," the winner of the Louis Vuitton Cup and the New Zealand defense reveal their boats, allowing the public to look at their designs.
Louis Vuitton also provides publicity for the America's Cup.

Challengers: 11
Nations: 7

Prada Challenge
Italy
Yacht Club Punta Ala
Patrizio Bertelli
Skipper: **Francesco de Angelis**
*Luna Rossa ITA 45**
Luna Rossa ITA 48
Architects: German Frers, Doug Peterson
Builder: Prada

AmericaOne
United States
St. Francis Yacht Club
Paul Cayard
Skipper: **Paul Cayard**
*AmericaOne USA 49**
*AmericaOne USA 61**
Architect: Bruce Nelson
Builder: Westerly Marine

Team Dennis Conner
United States
Cortez Racing Association
Dennis Conner
Skipper: **Ken Reid**
*Stars & Stripes USA 55**
Architects: Reichel-Pugh
Builder: New England Boatworks

Nippon Challenge
Japan
Nippon Yacht Club
Tatsumitsu Yamasaki
Skipper: **Peter Gilmour**
Asura JPN 44
*Idaten JPN 52**
Architect: Professeur Hideaki Miyata
Builder: NCBT

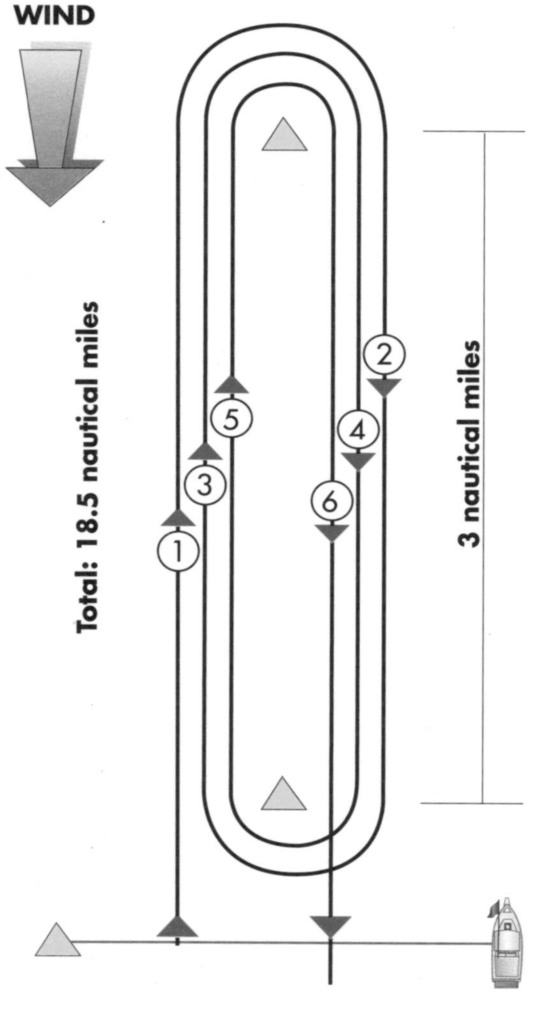

Auckland Circuit 2000
Drawing by François Chevalier

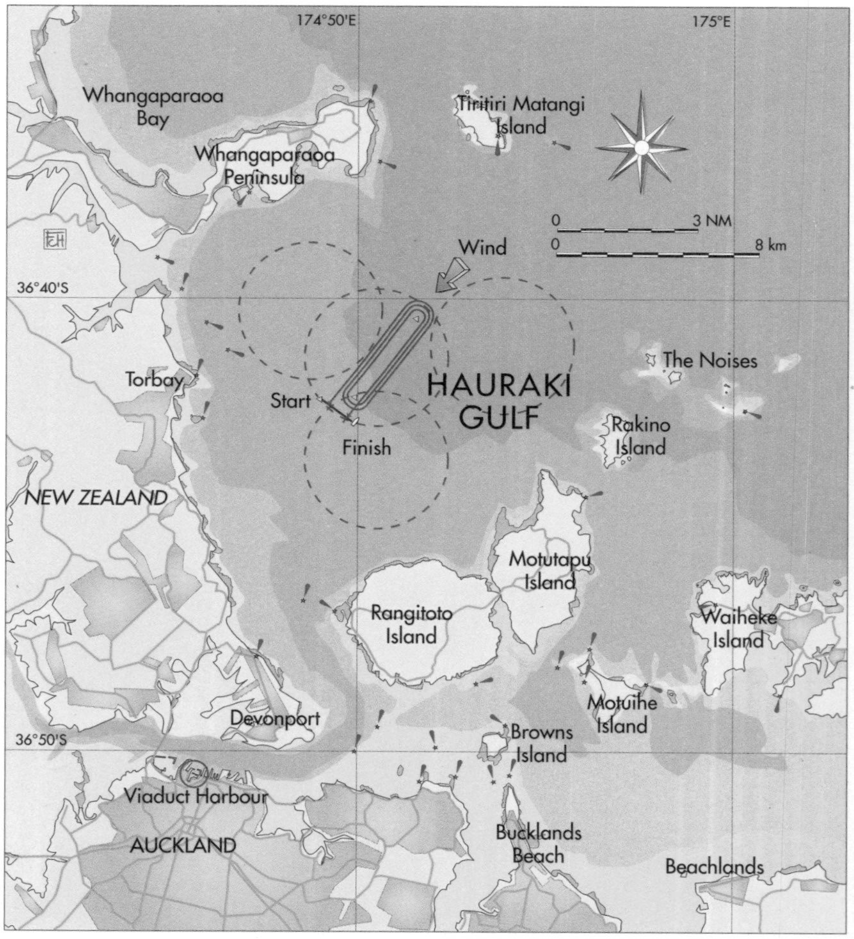

Auckland Chart 2000
Drawing by François Chevalier

America True
United States
San Francisco Yacht Club
Dawn Riley
Skipper: **John Cutler**
*America True USA 51**
Architect: Phil Kaiko
Builder: James Betts

Le Défi Bouygues Telecom-Transiciel
France
Union Nationale pour la Course au Large
Xavier de Lesquen
Skipper: **Bertrand Pacé**
*6e Sens FRA 46**
Architects: Daniel Andrieu, Bernard Nivelt
Builder: Multiplast

Young America
United States
New York Yacht Club
John Marshall
Skipper: **Ed Baird**
*Young America USA 53**
*Young America USA 58**
Architects: Bruce Farr, Duncan MacLane
Builder: Goetz Custom Boats

Spanish Challenge
Spain
Monte Real Club de Yates de Bayona
Real Club Nautica de Valencia
Pedro Campos
Skipper: **Pedro Campos, Luis Doreste**
*Bravo España ESP 47**
Bravo España ESP 56
Architects: Rolf Vrolijk, Javier Pamies
Builder: CADE

Aloha Racing
United States
Waikiki Yacht Club
James Andrews
Skipper: **John Kolius**
*Abracadabra USA 50**
*Abracadabra USA 54**
Architects: Dovell & Burns
Builder: Aloha Racing

Young Australia 2000
Australia
Cruising Yacht Club of Australia
Syd Fischer
Skipper: **James Spithill**
*Young Australia AUS 31**
*Young Australia AUS 29**
Architects: Fluid Thinking
Builder: John McConaghy

Fast 2000
Switzerland
Club Nautique de Morges
Marc Pajot
Skipper: **Marc Pajot**
*be hAPpy SUI 59**
Architects: Philippe Briand, Peter van Oossanen
Builder: Fast 2000

Luna Rossa ITA 45
Drawing by François Chevalier

5./ LOUIS VUITTON CUP RESULTS 1999–2000

Round Robin 1 – October 18 to 28, 1999

	Prada Challenge	AmericaOne	Young America	America True	Nippon Challenge	Spanish Challenge	Stars & Stripes	Aloha Racing	6ᵉ Sens	Young Australia 2000	be hAPpy	Points
Prada Challenge		•	•	•	•	•	•	•	•	•	•	10
AmericaOne				•	•	•	•	•	•	•	•	8
Young America		•		•	•	•		•	•	•	•	8
America True						•	•	•	•	•	•	6
Nippon Challenge				•		•		•	•	•	•	5.5
Spanish Challenge							•	•	•	•	•	5
Stars & Stripes			•		•				•	•	•	4.5
Aloha Racing							•		•	•	•	4
6ᵉ Sens										•	•	2
Young Australia 2000											•	1
be hAPpy												0

- *One point per win*
- *Half point subtracted for errors*

Round Robin 2 – November 6 to 20, 1999

	Prada Challenge	America True	Stars & Stripes	AmericaOne	Nippon Challenge	Young America	Spanish Challenge	Aloha Racing	6ᵉ Sens	Young Australia 2000	be hAPpy	Wins
Prada Challenge		•		•	•	•	•	•	•	•	•	9
America True			•	•	•		•	•	•	•	•	8
Stars & Stripes	•			•	•	•	•		•	•	•	8
AmericaOne					•	•	•	•	•	•	•	7
Nippon Challenge						•	•	•	•	•	•	6
Young America		•					•	•	•			4
Spanish Challenge									•	•	•	3
Aloha Racing			•				•			•		3
6ᵉ Sens								•		•	•	3
Young Australia 2000						•					•	2
be hAPpy						•		•				2

- *Four points per win*

Round Robin 3 – December 2 to 16, 1999

	Prada Challenge	Nippon Challenge	America True	AmericaOne	Stars & Stripes	6ᵉ Sens	Young America	Spanish Challenge	Aloha Racing	Young Australia 2000	be hAPpy	Wins	Points
Prada Challenge			•		•	•	•	•	•	•	dns	7	109
Nippon Challenge	•				•	•	•	•	•	•	•	8	101.5
America True		•		•	•		•		•	•	•	7	101
AmericaOne	•	•					•	•	•	•	•	7	99
Stars & Stripes				•			•		•	•	•	5	81.5
6ᵉ Sens			•	•	•		dns	•	•	•	•	7	77
Young America						dns		•	•	•	•	4	60
Spanish Challenge			•		•					•	•	4	53
Aloha Racing								•		•	•	3	43
Young Australia 2000											•	1	18
be hAPpy	dns											0	8

- *Nine points per win*
- dns: *Did not start*

Semifinals – January 2 to 14, 2000

	AmericaOne	Prada Challenge	Stars & Stripes	Nippon Challenge	America True	6ᵉ Sens	Points
AmericaOne		••	•	••	•	••	8
Prada Challenge			•	••	••	••	7
Stars & Stripes	•	•		••	•	••	6†
Nippon Challenge					••	••	4
America True	•		•				2
6ᵉ Sens					••		1.5

- *One point per win*
- *Half point subtracted for errors*
† *One point penalty*

Final – January 25 to February 6, 2000

	1	2	3	4	5	6	7	8	9	
Prada Challenge	•		•	•				•	•	5
AmericaOne		•			•	•	•			4

6./ AUCKLAND, NEW ZEALAND 2003

Conditions for the Louis Vuitton Cup, 2003

A Challenger of Record Committee is created among the challengers.
Sailboats: International America's Cup Class (IACC).
Qualifiers: Two round robins; quarterfinals, with a repechage; semifinals, also with a repechage; and finals, best out of five.
The number of boats built by each challenge is limited to two.
The challengers can modify or change their boat between two round robins.
The members of a challenge must have been residents of the country they represent for at least two years.
At the end of the Louis Vuitton Cup, "unveiling day," the winner and the New Zealand defense displays their boats, allowing the public to view them.
Louis Vuitton is the official timekeeper of the Louis Vuitton Cup.
Louis Vuitton also provides publicity for the America's Cup.

Challengers: 10
Nations: 7

Alinghi America's Cup 2003
Switzerland
Société Nautique de Genève
Ernesto Bertarelli
Skipper: **Russell Coutts**
*Alinghi SUI-64**
Alinghi SUI-75
Architect: Rolf Vrolijk
Builder: Decision SA

Prada Challenge
Italy
Yacht Club Punta Ala
Patrizio Bertelli
Skipper: **Francesco de Angelis**
*Luna Rossa ITA-74**
Luna Rossa ITA-80
Architects: German Frers, Doug Peterson, German Frers, Jr.
Builder: Prada, Green Marine

Oracle BMW Racing
United States
Golden Gate Yacht Club
Larry Ellison
Skippers: **John Cutler, Peter Holmberg**
Oracle BMW USA-71
*Oracle BMW USA-76**
Architect: Farr Yacht Design
Builder: Smyth and Gillies

OneWorld Challenge
United States
Seattle Yacht Club
Craig McCaw
Skipper: **Peter Gilmour**
OneWorld USA-65
*OneWorld USA-67**
Architects: Laurie Davidson, Bruce Nelson, Phil Kaiko
Builder: OneWorld Challenge

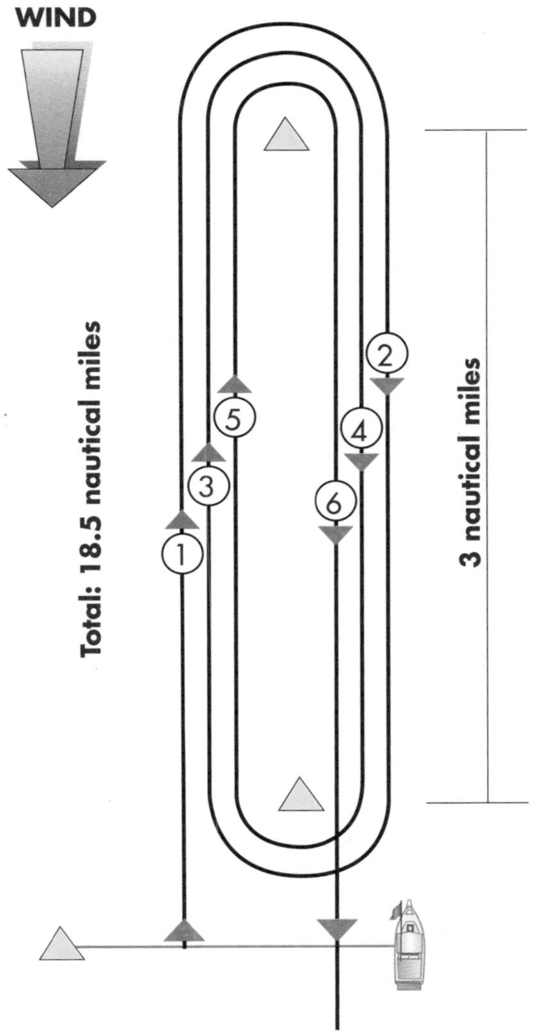

Auckland Circuit 2003
Drawing by François Chevalier

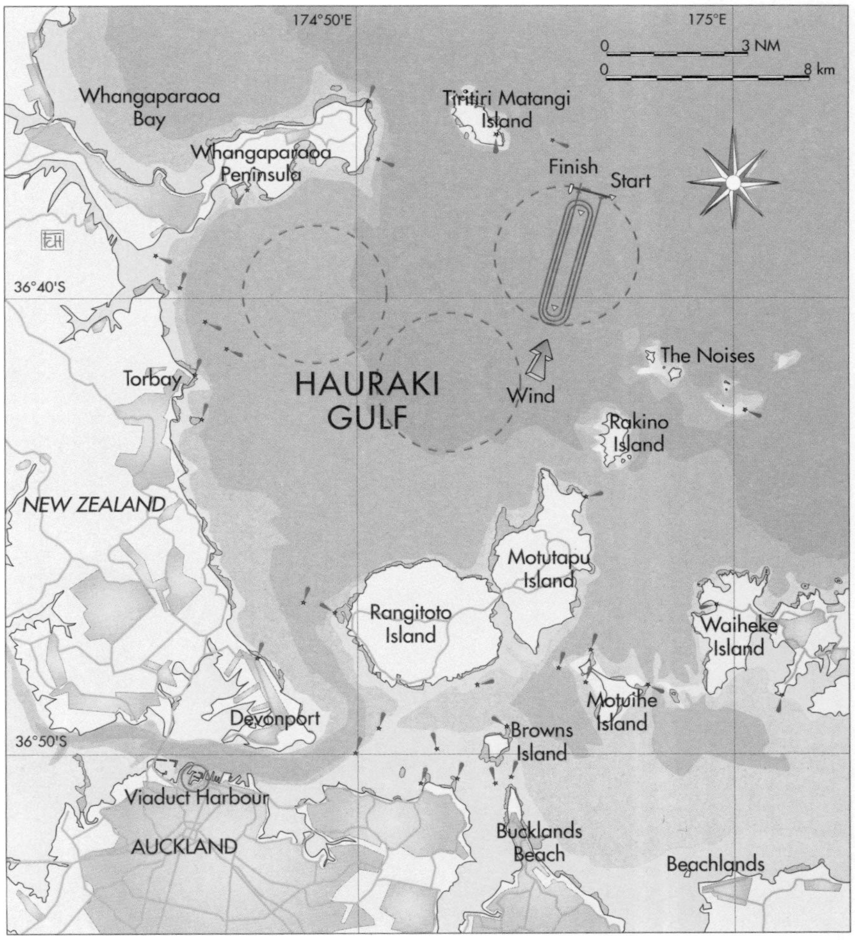

Auckland Chart 2003
Drawing by François Chevalier

Victory Challenge
Sweden
Gamla Stans Yacht Sällskap
Mats Johansson
Skipper: **Magnus Holmberg**
*Örn SWE 63**
*Örn SWE 73**
Architect: German Frers, Jr.
Builder: Chris Mellow

Team Dennis Conner
United States
New York Yacht Club
Dennis Conner
Skipper: **Ken Read**
*Stars & Stripes USA-66**
Stars & Stripes USA-77
Architect: Reichel-Pugh
Builder: New England Boatworks

GBR Challenge
United Kingdom
Royal Ocean Racing Club
Peter Harrison
Skipper: **Ian Walker**
*Wight Lightning GBR 70**
*Wight Magic GBR 78**
Architect: Derek Clark
Builder: Jason Akers, B. Linton

Le Défi Areva
France
Union Nationale pour la Course au Large
Xavier de Lesquen
Skipper: **Pierre Mas**
*Le Défi Areva FRA-69**
*Le Défi Areva FRA-79**
Architect: Yaka Design Team
Builder: Multiplast

Mascalzone Latino
Italy
Reale Yacht Club Canottieri Savoia
Vicenzo Onorato
Skipper: **Paolo Cian**
*Mascalzone Latino ITA-72**
Architect: Giovanni Ceccarelli
Builder: Tencara

Alinghi SUI 64
Drawing by François Chevalier

6./ LOUIS VUITTON CUP RESULTS 2002–2003

Round Robin 1 – October 1 to 14, 2002

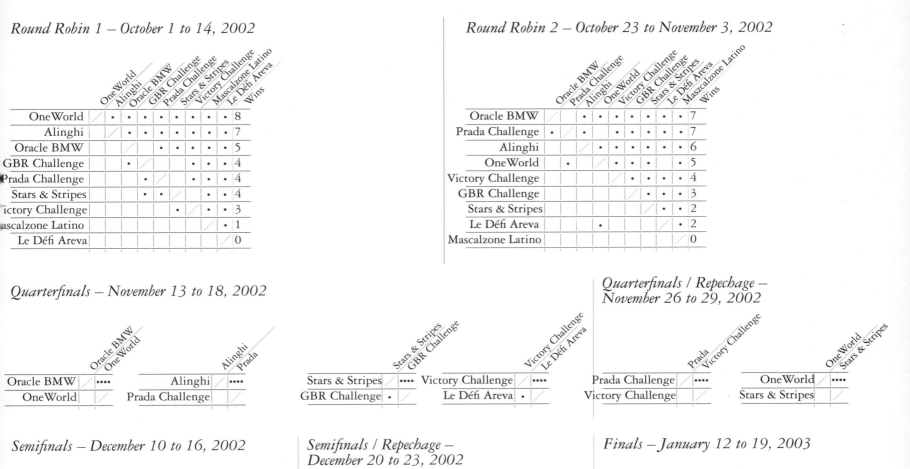

	OneWorld	Alinghi	Oracle BMW	GBR Challenge	Prada Challenge	Stars & Stripes	Victory Challenge	Mascalzone Latino	Le Défi Areva	Wins
OneWorld	/	•	•	•	•	•	•	•	•	8
Alinghi		/	•	•	•	•	•	•	•	7
Oracle BMW			/		•	•	•	•	•	5
GBR Challenge			•	/			•	•	•	4
Prada Challenge				•	/		•	•	•	4
Stars & Stripes				•	•	/		•	•	4
ictory Challenge						•	/	•	•	3
ascalzone Latino								/	•	1
Le Défi Areva									/	0

Round Robin 2 – October 23 to November 3, 2002

	Oracle BMW	Prada Challenge	Alinghi	OneWorld	Victory Challenge	GBR Challenge	Stars & Stripes	Le Défi Areva	Maszcalzone Latino	Wins
Oracle BMW	/		•	•	•	•	•	•	•	7
Prada Challenge	•	/	•		•	•	•	•	•	7
Alinghi			/	•	•	•	•	•	•	6
OneWorld		•		/	•	•	•		•	5
Victory Challenge					/	•	•	•	•	4
GBR Challenge						/	•	•	•	3
Stars & Stripes							/	•	•	2
Le Défi Areva				•				/	•	2
Mascalzone Latino									/	0

Quarterfinals – November 13 to 18, 2002

	Oracle BMW	OneWorld
Oracle BMW	/	••••
OneWorld		/

	Alinghi	Prada
Alinghi	/	••••
Prada Challenge		/

	Stars & Stripes	GBR Challenge
Stars & Stripes	/	••••
GBR Challenge	•	/

	Victory Challenge	Le Défi Areva
Victory Challenge	/	••••
Le Défi Areva	•	/

Quarterfinals / Repechage – November 26 to 29, 2002

	Prada	Victory Challenge
Prada Challenge	/	••••
Victory Challenge		/

	OneWorld	Stars & Stripes
OneWorld	/	••••
Stars & Stripes		/

Semifinals – December 10 to 16, 2002

	Alinghi	Oracle BMW
Alinghi	/	••••
Oracle BMW		/

	OneWorld	Prada
OneWorld	/	••••
Prada Challenge	••	/

Semifinals / Repechage – December 20 to 23, 2002

	Oracle BMW	OneWorld
Oracle BMW	/	••••
OneWorld		/

Finals – January 12 to 19, 2003

	1	2	3	4	5	6	
Alinghi	•	•	•		•	•	5
Oracle BMW				•			1

7./ MARSEILLE, FRANCE VALENCIA, SPAIN MALMÖ, SWEDEN TRAPANI, ITALY 2007

Conditions for the Louis Vuitton Cup, 2004–2007

An organization for the entire event, under the control of the defender: AC Management
Challenger of Record: Golden Gate Yacht Club.
Sailboats: International America's Cup Class (IACC)

Formula:

$$\frac{L + 1.25\sqrt{S} - 98\sqrt[3]{D}}{0.677} = 24 \text{ meter}$$

L = rated length in meters
S = rated sail area in square meters
D = displacement in cubic meters
L and S are limited by new annexed formulas

The maximum beam is 4.5 meters.
The maximum draft is 4.1 meters.
The displacement is 24 tons.
Carbon construction, hull and mast.
Maximum height of mast is 32.5 meters.
17 crew members and one guest.

Qualifiers: 13 Louis Vuitton Acts, two round robins, semifinals, and finals, best of five. The odd-numbered Acts are a series of fleet regattas. The defender participates in the Acts.
Each challenge can acquire two sailboats and build two. The challengers can modify (up to 50%) or change their boat between two round robins. At the beginning of 2006, all America's Class boats must conform to the new design rule.
An architect can only work for one challenge.
The nationality rule is softened; it is enough to be part of the team for eighteen months.
April 1, 2007, is "unveiling day," when the competitors show their boats to the public.
Louis Vuitton is the official timekeeper of the Louis Vuitton Cup.
Louis Vuitton also provides world coverage for the America's Cup.

Challengers: 11
Nations: 9

Emirates Team New Zealand
New Zealand
Royal New Zealand Yacht Squadron
Grant Dalton
Skipper: **Dean Barker**
Team New Zealand NZL 81
*Team New Zealand NZL 82**
*Team New Zealand NZL 84**
*Team New Zealand NZL 92**
Architects: Andy Claughton, ETNZ Team Design
Builder: Cookson's Boatyard, Auckland

Luna Rossa Challenge
Italy
Yacht Club Italiano
Patrizio Bertelli
Skipper: **Francesco de Angelis**
*Luna Rossa ITA 74**
Luna Rossa ITA 80
*Luna Rossa ITA 86**
*Luna Rossa ITA 94**
Architects: Bruce Nelson, Claudio Maletto
Builder: Persico, Nembro

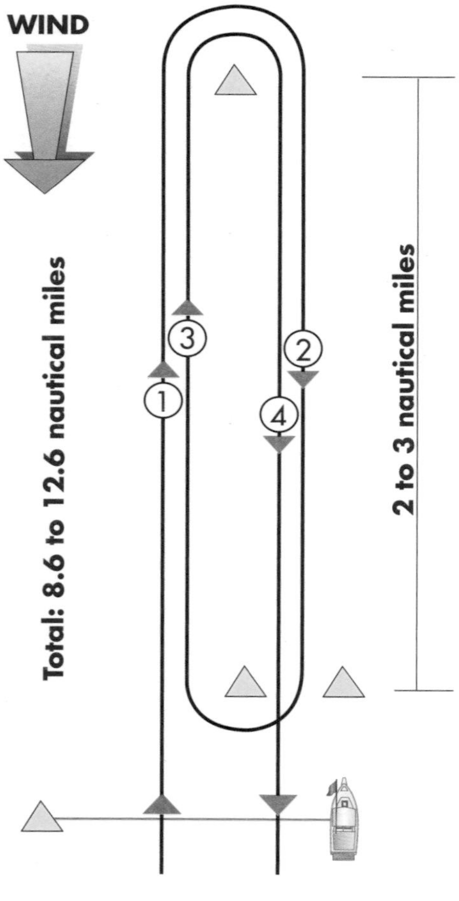

Circuit Valencia 2007
Drawing by François Chevalier

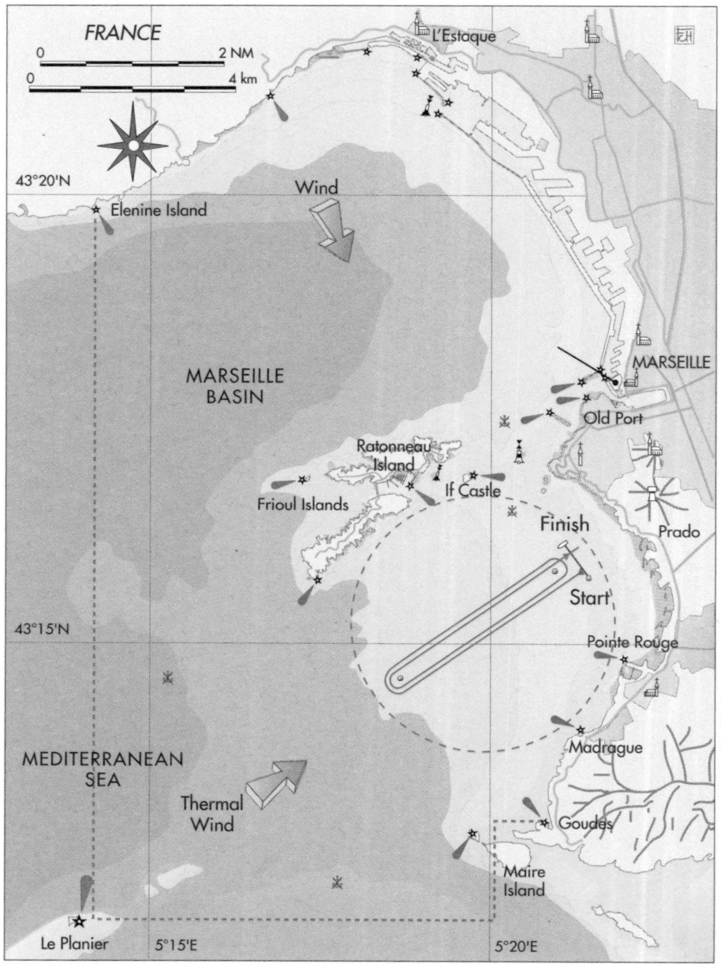

Marseille Chart 2004
Drawing by François Chevalier

BMW Oracle Racing
United States
Golden Gate Yacht Club
Larry Ellison
Skipper: **Chris Dickson**
BMW Oracle USA 71
*BMW Oracle USA 76**
*BMW Oracle USA 87**
*BMW Oracle USA 98**
Architects: Bruce Farr, Ian Burns, Juan Kouyoumdjian
Builder: BMW Oracle Racing, Anacortes

Desafío Español 2007
Spain
Real Federation Espanola de Vela
Augustin Zulueta
Skipper: **Luis Doreste**
Desafío Español ESP 65
*Desafío Español ESP 67**
*Desafío Español ESP 88**
*Desafío Español ESP 97**
Architects: Reichel-Pugh
Builder: King Marine Boatyard, Alginet

Mascalzone Latino–Capitalia Team
Italy
Reale Yacht Club Canottieri Savoia
Vicenzo Onorato
Skipper: **Vasco Vascotto**
Mascalzone Latino ITA 66
*Mascalzone Latino ITA 77**
*Mascalzone Latino ITA 90**
*Mascalzone Latino ITA 99**
Architect: Harry Dunning
Builder: Marine Composite, Andora

Victory Challenge
Sweden
Gamla Stans Yacht Sällskap
Hugo Stenbeck
Skipper: **Magnus Holmberg**
*Örn SWE 63**
*Örn SWE 73**
*Järv SWE 96**
Architects: German Frers and German Frers, Jr.
Builder: Victory C.'s Yard, Linholmen

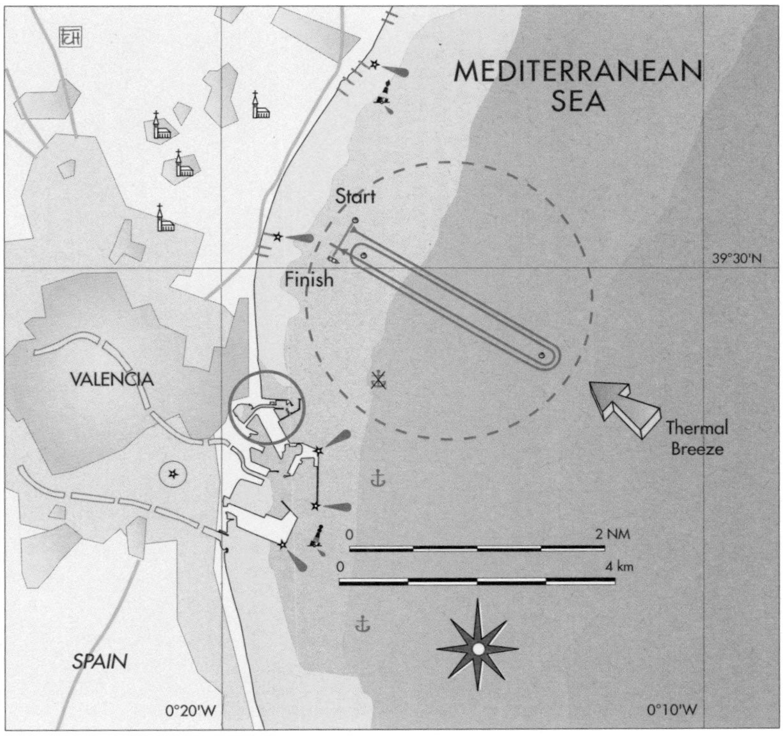

Valencia Chart 2004–2007
Drawing by François Chevalier

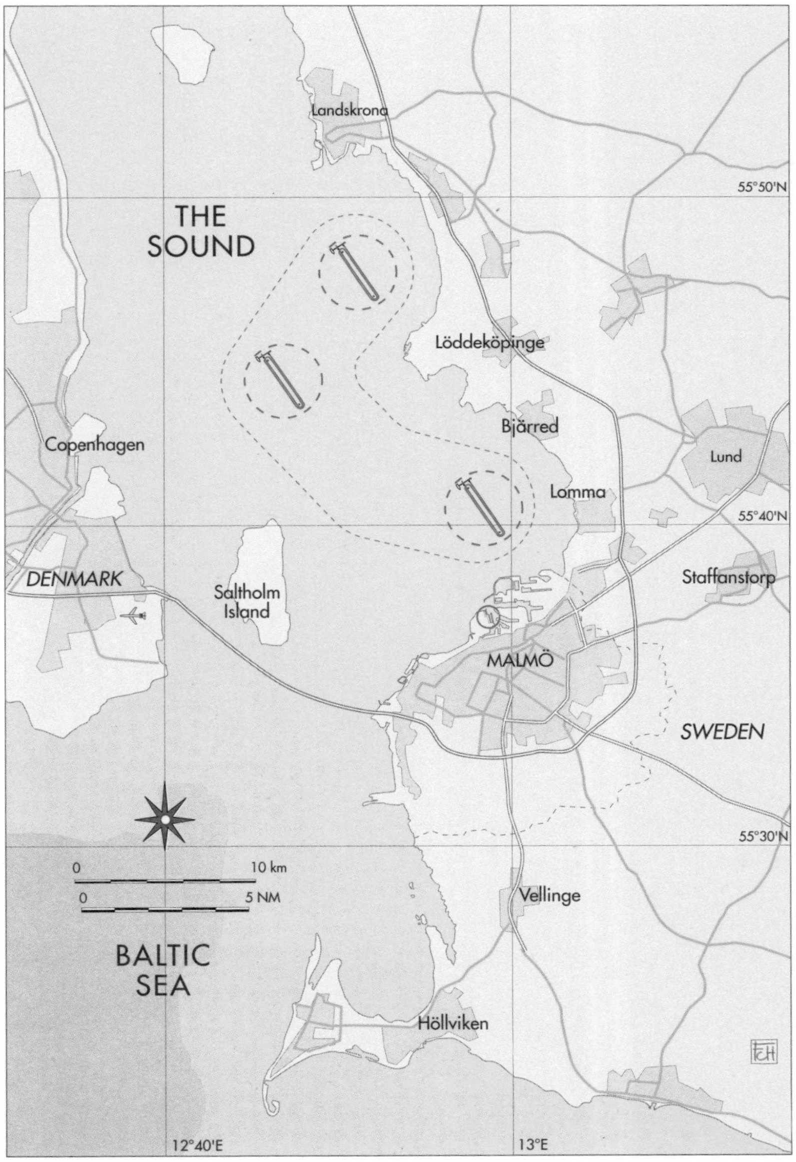

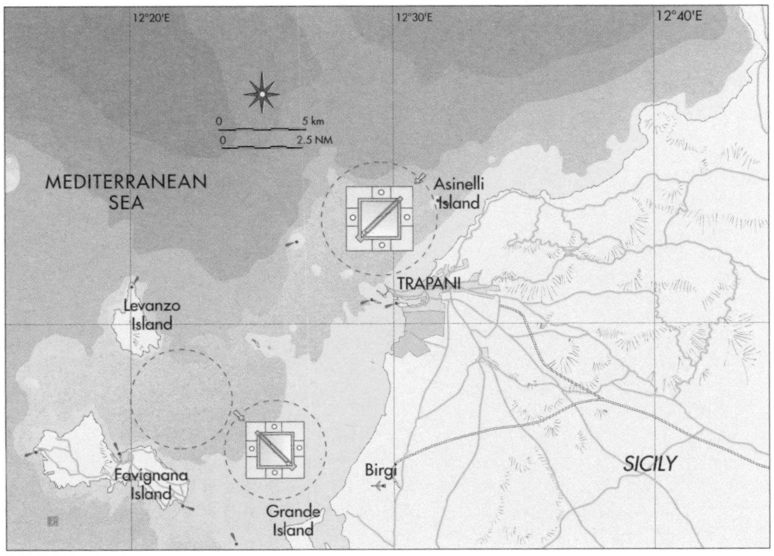

Trapani Chart 2005
Drawing by François Chevalier

Malmö Chart 2005
Drawing by François Chevalier

Team Shosholoza
South Africa
Royal Cape Yacht Club
Salvatore Sarno
Skippers: **Ian Ainslie, Geoff Meek**
Shosholoza RSA 48
*Shosholoza RSA 83**
Architects: Jason Ker
Builder: Shosholoza Boatyards, Cape Town

Areva Challenge
France
Cercle de la Voile de Paris
Stéphane Kandler
Skippers: **Thierry Peponnet, Sébastian Col**
*K-Challenge FRA 57**
*K-Challenge/Areva FRA 60**
*Areva FRA 93**
Architects: Bernard Nivelt, Dimitri Nicolopoulos
Builder: Composite Works, La Ciota

+39 Challenge
Italy
Circolo Vela Gargnano
Lorenzo Rizzardi
Skipper: **Luca Devoti**
*+39 ITA 59**
*+39 ITA 85**
Architect: Giovanni Ceccarelli
Builder: Soleri Boatyards, Ravenne

United Internet Team Germany
Germany
Deutscher Challenger Yacht Club
Michael Scheeren
Skipper: **Jesper Bank**
*United I Team Germany GER 72**
*United I Team Germany GER 89**
Architect: Alex Mohnhaupt
Builder: Knierim Werft, Kiel

China Team
China
Qingdao International Yacht Club
Chaoyang Wang
Skipper: **Pierre Mas**
*CHN 69**
*CHN 79**
Longtze CHN 95*
Architects: Daniel Andrieu, Hervé Devaux
Builder: McConaghy International, Dong Guan

Team New Zealand NZL 92
Drawing by François Chevalier

7./ LOUIS VUITTON CUP RESULTS 2004–2007

Louis Vuitton Acts from September 5, 2004 to April 7, 2007

	LV Act 1 - Sept. 5–11, 2004 Marseille	LV Act 2 - Oct. 5–12, 2004 Valencia	LV Act 3 - Oct. 14–17, 2004 Valencia	Points	Ranking 2004	LV Act 4 - Jun. 16–22, 2005 Valencia	LV Act 5 - Jun. 24–26, 2005 Valencia	LV Act 6 - Aug. 25–31, 2005 Malmö	LV Act 7 - Sept. 2–4, 2005 Malmö	LV Act 8 - Sept. 29–Oct. 5, 2005 Trapani	LV Act 9 - Oct. 7–9, 2005 Trapani	Points	Ranking 2005	LV Act 10 - May 11–17, 2006 Valencia	LV Act 11 - May 19–21, 2006 Valencia	LV Act 12 - Jun. 22–Jul. 2, 2006 Valencia	Points	Ranking 2006	LV Act 13 - Apr. 3–7, 2007 Valencia	Points	Ranking 2007	Ranking LV acts
Alinghi	2	4	1	7	3	1	2	1	1	1	1	71	1	4	1	2	32	2	1		1	1
Emirates Team NZ	3	1	2	6	1	2	3	3	4	2	3	61	2	3	3	1	32	1	2	33	2	2
BMW Oracle Racing	1	3	3	7	2	3	4	2	2	4	2	61	3	1	4	3	31	3	5	24	5	3
Luna Rossa Challenge		2	4	13	4	4	1	4	3	3	6	57	4	2	2	4	31	4	4	27	4	4
Desafío Español 2007						6	8	5	5	8	4	42	5	5	9	5	20	6	6	21	6	5
Mazcalzone Latino–CT						8	5	7	9	9	10	30	9	7	5	6	21	5	3	30	3	6
Victory Challenge						5	6	8	11	6	8	34	6	6	10	7	16	8	8	15	8	7
Team Shosholoza	6	8	7	21	7	12	12	11	10	10	5	18	11	8	6	8	17	7	7	18	7	8
Areva Challenge	5	6	5	16	6	7	7	9	6	5	12	32	7	10	7	9	13	9	9	12	9	9
+39 Challenge		7	8	22	8	9	9	6	8	7	7	32	8	9	8	10	12	10	11	6	11	10
UI Team Germany						10	10	10	7	11	9	21	10	11	11	12	6	11	10	9	10	11
China Team / Le Défi						11	11	12	12	12	11	9	12	12	12	12	3	12	12	3	12	12

Round Robin 1 – April 16 to 28, 2007

	BMW Oracle Racing	Luna Rossa Challenge	Emirates Team NZ	Desafío Español 2007	Mazcalzone Latino–CT	Victory Challenge	Team Shosholoza	Areva Challenge	+39 Challenge	UI Team Germany	China Team	Points	Total points
BMW Oracle Racing	/	•	•		•	•	•	•	•	•	•	18	21
Luna Rossa Challenge		/	•	•	•	•		•	•	•	•	16	19
Emirates Team NZ			/	•		•	•	•	•	•	•	14	18
Desafío Español 2007	•			/	•	•	•		•	•	•	14	17
Mazcalzone Latino–CT			•		/		•	•	•	•	•	12	14
Victory Challenge					•	/	•	•	•	•	•	12	14
Team Shosholoza		•					/	•	•	•	•	10	12
Areva Challenge				•			dnf	/	•	•	•	8	9
+39 Challenge									/	•	•	4	6
UI Team Germany										/	•	2	3
China Team			dns		dnf			dns	dns		/	0	1

- *Two points per win*
- dnf: *Did not finish*
- dns: *Did not start*

Round Robin 2 – April 29 to May 9, 2007

	Emirates Team NZ	BMW Oracle Racing	Luna Rossa Challenge	Desafío Español 2007	Mazcalzone Latino–CT	Victory Challenge	Team Shosholoza	Areva Challenge	+39 Challenge	UI Team Germany	China Team	Points	Total points
Emirates Team NZ	/	•	•	•	•	•	•	•	•	•	•	20	38
BMW Oracle Racing		/	•	•	•	•	•	•	•	•		16	37
Luna Rossa Challenge			/	•	•	•	•	•	•	•	•	16	35
Desafío Español 2007				/	•		•	•	•	•	•	12	29
Mazcalzone Latino–CT					/	•			•	•	•	8	22
Victory Challenge			•			/	•	•	•	•	•	12	26
Team Shosholoza				•			/	•		•	•	8	20
Areva Challenge				•				/	•	•	•	8	17
+39 Challenge						•			/	•	•	6	12
UI Team Germany										/	•	2	5
China Team		•									/	2	3

- *Two points per win*

Semifinals – May 14 to 23, 2007

	1	2	3	4	5	6	7	
Emirates Team NZ	•	•		•	•		•	5
Desafío Español 2007			•			•		2

	1	2	3	4	5	6	
Luna Rossa Challenge	•		•	•	•	•	5
BMW Oracle Racing		•					1

Finals – June 1 to 12, 2007

	1	2	3	4	5	
Emirates Team NZ	•	•	•	•	•	5
Luna Rossa Challenge						0

BIOGRAPHIES

Francesco de Angelis

Born in Naples on September 11, 1960, Francesco de Angelis was initiated into sailing by his father when he was fifteen. In 1985, he abandoned his studies to dedicate himself to sailing keelboats as well as racing offshore. A five-time world champion—in the J-24 (1987), the One Ton (1989 and 1992), and the ILC 40 (1995 and 1996)—he led the Italian team to victory in the Admiral's Cup in 1995.

An imposing man at six foot four, elegant and reserved, de Angelis made a name for himself as a great skipper of the Cup through his talent and his unfailing sangfroid. Victor at the helm of the *Luna Rossa* in the 2000 Louis Vuitton Cup in a series of memorable regattas, he was fourth in 2003 and a finalist in 2007.

Dean Barker

At twenty-four, New Zealander Dean Barker, a pillar of New Zealand's 2000 defense as skipper of the team's training boat, won his first America's Cup when Russell Coutts allowed him to take the helm for the fifth and final match.

Barker was born on April 18, 1973, in Auckland, where his father owned the men's store Barker's Clothing. Dean early on sailed an Optimist dinghy, then competed in the P-class, the 470, the Laser, in which he was a world youth champion, and the Finn. After leaving Russell Coutts, he took command of Team New Zealand's defense for 2003, but was beaten by his old mentor. In 2007, in Valencia, on the Emirates Team New Zealand, he won the Louis Vuitton Cup but lost (5–2) to the defender *Alinghi* by only a tiny second in the seventh and last match—a second that Barker won't soon forget. He'll be back!

Christine Bélanger

Born in Paris on August 20, 1956, Christine Bélanger studied physical chemistry in the United States. On her return to Paris, she studied languages and worked from 1981 as public relations officer for Christian Dior Parfums. She took on Möet & Chandon at the time when the prestigious champagne brand became associated with the America's Cup, in 1986. Bélanger then joined Jour J, founded by Bruno Troublé, before taking on the directorship of the events for Louis Vuitton beginning in 1991. A great traveler, director of the Louis Vuitton Cup since 1998, she unfailingly looks after Louis Vuitton commitments in the America's Cup and organizes the parties and Classic Awards that the house of Vuitton holds all over the world.

Ernesto Bertarelli

Born September 22, 1965, Ernesto Bertarelli received his MBA from Harvard. As head of his father's pharmaceutical company, La Serono, which rapidly flourished under him, he is among the five richest people in Switzerland.

A passionate sailor since he was a child, Bertarelli has participated in a number of regattas as helmsman, navigator, or crew member. His achievements speak for themselves: first in the Sardinia Cup in 1998, third at Fastnet 1999, holder of five victories in the Bol d'Or (1997, 2000, 2001, 2002, and 2003), world champion in the Farr 40 in 2001, and victor of the Swedish Match Cup in 2002. He was also a crew member on the winning team for the Louis Vuitton Cup and the America's Cup in 2003. The New Zealand "Dream Team" in large part contributed to his two victories. Managing the organization of the 2007 race as his own business, he transformed the event, in the process greatly increasing its budget. As victor and defender, the protocol he imposed on the next America's Cup provoked a general uproar and caused Louis Vuitton to break off its relationship with the race, complaining that it was becoming too commercial.

Patrizio Bertelli

Head of the Prada Challenge, which won the 2000 Louis Vuitton Cup in Auckland with the *Luna Rossa,* he came in fourth in 2003, won the Louis Vuitton Act 5 fleet racing in Valencia in 2005, and reached the finals of the 2007 Louis Vuitton Cup. Patrizio Bertelli has invested heavily in the America's Cup.

Born in Arezzo, Tuscany, in 1946, into a family of lawyers, Bertelli is a competent, creative, and detail-loving man. Having earned a degree in engineering, he created his own company in 1967. Ten years later, he joined up with Muccia Prada to create the luxury goods manufacturer Prada, beginning a fantastic success story. Today, his investment in the Louis Vuitton Cup is his great indulgence, and certainly the rewards have been substantial. He has always loved to navigate, and adores classic yachts.

John Bertrand

Born to Win, the title of Bertrand's book, sums it up: he claimed the America's Cup for Australia after 132 years of American supremacy, a historic exploit that made him a national hero. Down 1 to 3 in that famous 1983 final, he came back to win 4 to 3.

Bertrand was born on December 20, 1946, in Chelsea, near Melbourne, Australia. He has always been a sailor. He was Australian champion in 1964, bronze medalist in the Finn class in the 1976 Summer Olympics in Montreal, second to Jim Hardy in the 1980 America's Cup, and was chosen by Alan Bond to be helmsman for the *Australia II* in 1983. In 1995, in San Diego, Bertrand returned to service on oneAustralia as skipper, with Rod Davis at the helm, but the best of their IACC boats, *AUS 35,* broke in two dramatically in the fourth round robin, shattering their chances of victory. They finished second in the Louis Vuitton Cup.

Marcel Bich

Marcel Bich was born in Turin on July 29, 1914. He was ten years old when his family emigrated to France. While he was still at school, his father died prematurely, and Marcel began to work for an ink maker. At the age of twenty-one, he bought a factory in the suburbs of Paris, and five years later he launched the Bic pen. It was a great success. In 1973, he developed a disposable lighter, and then, two years later, the Bic razor.

In September 1967, Baron Marcel Bich launched the first French challenge for the 1970 America's Cup. The New York Yacht Club told him that he would have to wait until 1973, as Australia had already issued a challenge. Determined to prevail, he relentlessly—and successfully—lobbied the Americans to modify the rules to allow a duel between the challengers. This historic decision revolutionized the America's Cup—henceforth, all challenges launched in the thirty days after the last regatta of the America's Cup would be accepted—and led to the creation of the Louis Vuitton Cup, in 1983.

From 1965 to 1979, Bich acquired a fleet of three 12-meters—the *Sovereign,* the *Constellation,* and the *Kurrewa*—and had two other ships built, the *Chancegger* and the *France I.* The last of these participated in the challenger's selections in 1970, 1974, and 1977 without success. The *France II,* put into the water in 1977, proved less speedy than the *France I.* For 1980, Bich asked architect Johan Valentijn to design the *France III,* which, with Bruno Troublé as skipper, made it to the challenger's finals but was beaten by the Australians 4 to 1. The man who showed the French yachtsmen the road to the America's Cup died in 1994.

Sir Peter Blake

Born in Auckland, New Zealand, on October 1, 1948, Peter Blake took up sailing at the age of five and never stopped. He has about 600,000 miles under his belt, most of them racing miles.

An engineer, private pilot, yachtsman, and adventurer, Blake organized as much as he sailed. Ten times named World Sailor of the Year, and knighted by the Queen of England in 1995, Sir Peter Blake managed a double victory for his country in the America's Cup, in 1995 and 2000. Winner of the Whitbread Round the World in 1989 on the *Steinlager,* and of the Jules Verne Trophy in 1994 on the *Enza,* he has taken part in every ocean race at some time or another.

Sir Peter Blake died during a pirate attack while navigating the Amazon on December 6, 2001.

Alan Bond

Born in London on April 22, 1938, Alan Bond was twelve when his family emigrated to Fremantle, Australia. Bond built his fortune in real estate, then invested in other areas, such as the brewing industry, gold mines, and the media. Between 1974 and 1980, he financed the Australian yachts *Southern Cross* and *Australia,* both of which won the challenger's selections for the America's Cup.

In 1983, Bond bankrolled the *Australia II,* which won the first Louis Vuitton Cup, then the America's Cup, ending 132 years of American domination. President of the defense for the following race, in 1987, he constructed two 12-meter boats, the *Australia III* and the *Australia IV,* which ran aground in the selection regattas.

Because of problems relating to the stock market crash of 1987 and some business deals he was involved in during 1995 and 1996, Bond was charged with corporate fraud and spent three years in prison before getting back on his feet.

Malin Burnham

"Put it in the bank!" Returning to San Diego after the victory of the *Stars & Stripes* over the *Kookaburra III,* Malin Burnham, himself director of a bank, couldn't think of a better place to keep the America's Cup safe.

As a child, Burnham debuted on the *Starlet,* a small Star class boat, at the San Diego Yacht Club. At seventeen, in 1946, he became the youngest Star world champion, with Lowell North as his team member. Skipper of the *Enterprise* during the defender's selections in 1977, Burnham was helmsman during the campaigns of the *Freedom* in 1980 and the *Liberty* in 1983. President of Dennis Conner's defense team, Sail America Foundation, in 1987, he headed the America's Cup organizing committee for 1992.

Pedro Campos

The 1992 commemoration of the five hundredth anniversary of Columbus's discovery of America struck Pedro Campos, the skipper of the *España 92 ESP-22,* as a lucky coincidence. "It is a great occasion for Spain to launch a challenge in the America's Cup," he explained.

Pedro Campos Calvo Sotelo was born in Cuntis, Galicia, on March 6, 1955. He learned to sail from his father and first raced at the age of ten, at the Club Nautico Sangenjo. Three years later, he won his first national title in the *Snipe.* He acquired seven world championships between 1976 and 1992.

As skipper of the *España 92,* then the *Rioja de España* three years later in 1995, Campos was remarkable in his mastery of the pre-start. In 2000, in Auckland, he yielded the helm to multiple Olympic champion Luis Blanco Doreste.

Yves Carcelle

A brilliant polytechnician, graduate of the international graduate business school INSEAD in France, and rigorous administrator, Yves Carcelle is also a lover of the good life. Born in 1948, he began his career with Spontex and Absorba; then, at the beginning of 1985, he became director of Descamps. In 1989 he entered the LVMH group. The following year, he was named president and CEO of Louis Vuitton Malletier, to which he brought a more modern, international outlook, adding creativity and innovation to the venerable company's reputation for luxury and quality.

Yves Carcelle is passionate about the America's Cup and the Louis Vuitton Cup, to which he has been unflaggingly devoted. He was struck at once by the very strong ties that for more than 150 years have unified the two legends that are the America's Cup and Louis Vuitton. "I believe that some locations and events have their own magic," he has said. "In this case, if you look at the America's Cup, how it was born, how it was kept by the Americans for so long, how the tycoons risked their money, their reputations, and their time for years to get it... all of this all makes it one of the most unique stories in the world." Handing over the trophy to the winner is a great moment for him. Thanks to him, the Louis Vuitton Cup has had the patronage of a venerable house.

Paul Cayard

"Anything is possible," Paul Cayard said of the Spanish challenge in 2007. Cayard has proved this to be true many times over at the helm of the sailboats he has led to victory. Some might call him lucky, but as his father, a French immigrant to the United States, said, "Whatever you do, be the best in the world." Paul took him at his word, as his race record shows.

Born on March 19, 1959, in San Francisco, Cayard began sailing at an early age. Introduced by his mentor Tom Blackaller to the Star class, he soon collected seven world championships: the Star and Maxi classes in 1988, the One Ton Cup in 1989, the America's Cup and 50-foot classes in 1991, the ILC-40 class in 1996, and finally the IMS class in 2000. In 1998 he became the first American to win the Whitbread Round the World, aboard the Swedish yacht *EF Language.* His America's Cup experience began in 1983, as mainsail trimmer on the 12-meter *Defender USA 33*; he was tactician on the *USA II* in 1987. Victor of the 1992 Louis Vuitton Cup on the *Il Moro di Venezia V,* he won the Citizen Cup in 1995. In 2000, he mounted his own challenge with the *AmericaOne,* which made it to the Louis Vuitton Cup finals.

Dennis Conner

Four-time winner of the America's Cup (1974, 1980, 1983, and 1988), Dennis Conner has also lost twice, in 1983 and 1995. With nine campaigns in twenty-nine years and around fifty matches won, it is no wonder that Dennis Conner has the nickname "Mr. America's Cup."

Dennis was born in San Diego on September 16, 1942, and devoted himself to his passion as a boy. At eleven, he became a member of the San Diego Yacht Club, where in 1984 he became the commodore. After finishing his studies at San Diego State University, he ran a small drapery firm before making sailing his vocation. Bronze medalist in the 1977 Olympics on the *Tempest,* he was two-time world champion on the *Star,* and earned seven national and international championships on *Etchells.* "When I'm on the water, I am at peace and almost always happy," Conner says, "especially when I'm winning!" Conner is a master of the aggressive pre-start, with a sixth sense for precisely judged time and distance.

Russell Coutts

Three-time winner of the America's Cup (1995, 2000, and 2003), gold medalist in the Finn single-handed dinghy in the 1984 Atlanta Olympics, three-time match racing world champion, Farr 40 and 12-meter world champion, and twice World Sailor of the Year: Russell Coutts is a prodigy of yacht racing!

Born in Wellington, New Zealand, on March 1, 1962, Coutts began sailing at the age of six and won his first regatta at nine. In 1987, he served as tactician on the 12-meter *New Zealand KZ 3* for the world championships, but he chose to complete his engineering studies rather than race in that year's America's Cup. In 2000, in Auckland, having won four consecutive races against the challenger the *Luna Rossa ITA 45,* he handed the helm over to his young understudy Dean Barker for the last and winning regatta, with a generosity that made him a national hero. In 2003, he won the Louis Vuitton Cup and then the America's Cup aboard the *Alinghi.* The following year, as a result of a dispute with the Swiss syndicate head Ernesto Bertarelli about his duties and the new America's Cup protocol, he was ousted. Coutts took advantage of the situation to develop a new light-displacement "one design" forty-four-foot boat, the *RC 44.* In 2007, at the end of the competition at Valencia, he returned to the side of the challengers, joining the American BMW Oracle Racing team.

Laurie Davidson

"If you had seen the faces of the people I showed my plan to . . ." Yacht architect Laurie Davidson loves to surprise—and to win, as he did with the innovative knuckle bow and "millennium rig" of the *Team New Zealand NZL 60,* which not only won the America's Cup 2000, but served as a yacht design benchmark for years to come.

Born in Dargaville, northwest of Auckland, New Zealand, in 1927, Davidson was passionate about sailing. His first design, the *Myth,* made when he was twenty, was a success. Davidson's boats have sailed four times in the America's Cup or Louis Vuitton Cup: in 1987, he was codesigner of the 12-meter "Kiwi Magic"; in 1995, of the victorious *Black Magic NZL 32*; and in 2000, of the *Team New Zealand NZL 60.* In 2003, he went into partnership with Bruce Nelson and Phil Kaiko for the challenger *OneWorld* from the Seattle Yacht Club, which reached the Louis Vuitton Cup finals. In 2007, he was nominated into the America's Cup Hall of Fame.

Chris Dickson

Chris Dickson, born on November 3, 1961, has always been on the water. The son of a renowned yachtsman in Auckland, New Zealand, he first experienced match racing aboard his father's sailboat. Junior World Champion in 1978, 1979, and 1980, and three-time world champion, he is famous for his aggressive starts.

In the 1987 Louis Vuitton Cup, the twenty-four-year-old Dickson skippered the plastic-hulled 12-meter *New Zealand,* dubbed the "Kiwi Magic." He trounced the opposition, with 37 victories in 38 matches, but Dennis Conner beat him 5 to 1 in the finals. At the helm of Japan's *Nippon* in 1992 in San Diego, he dominated the first three round robins, but finished third in the semifinals. In 1995, as owner, skipper, and helmsman of the *Tag Heuer NZL 39,* Dickson ran a superb race and came in third again. He made it to the finals of the Louis Vuitton Cup in 2003 on the *Oracle BMW,* but only to the semifinals in 2007 for BMW Oracle Racing—a disappointing result considering the wealth of ability of his team, which resulted in his replacement by Russell Coutts.

Larry Ellison

To talk about Larry Ellison, you have to use hyperbole: the man is larger than life, with his flamboyance, his four marriages, his cars, fighter planes, estates, and yachts. Born in the Bronx on August 17, 1944, he was left at nine months by his young mother with an aunt in Chicago, where he grew up. On leaving college, Laurence Joseph Ellison took a chance developing a systems software program, Oracle, which made his fortune.

During his first campaign in the America's Cup 2003, Ellison recruited five of the best for his America's Cup team—Bruce Farr, who designed both *Oracle BMW USA 71* and *USA 76,* along with Paul Cayard, John Cutler, Chris Dickson, and Peter Holmberg—which made the Louis Vuitton finals, though Cayard and Cutler dropped out along the way. In 2007, Chris Dickson gave him carte blanche; his *BMW Oracle* came in first in Act 1 in Marseille and Act 10 in Valencia, but he was beaten in the semifinal.

In the wake of the *Alinghi*'s victory and the ensuing controversy over the conditions the Swiss club imposed on the next America's Cup, Ellison's BMW Oracle Racing lodged a surprise challenge, with the goal of forcing a renegotiation for a fairer rule for challengers.

Laurent Esquier

Laurent Esquier was born in 1953 in Batna at the foot of the mountains in Algeria. His experience in the America's Cup is without equal.

Crew member aboard the boat of Baron Bich in 1974 and 1977, Esquier coordinated the construction of the *France III* in 1980. Crossing over to the side of the American defense in 1983, he joined the crew of the *Freedom,* which served as pacemaker for the *Liberty,* Dennis Conner's sailboat. In Australia, Esquier became trainer for the New Zealanders, who reached the finals of the Louis Vuitton Cup. He stayed with Michael Fay in 1988, during the epoch of the "Big Boat." In 1992 in San Diego, he organized the coordination of Raul Gardini's *Il Moro di Venezia,* victor of the Louis Vuitton Cup. For the following race, Esquier worked for the challenger Chris Dickson as manager of the *Tag Heuer.* In Auckland, in 2000 and 2003, he was operations manager for Prada Challenge, Bertelli's defender. He joined the BMW Oracle Racing team in April 2004.

Bruce Farr

If you ask Bruce Farr how long he has been designing boats, he'll answer, "Well before I was born!" Farr was born on May 17, 1949, in the bay of Auckland, New Zealand. His father was a sailboat builder, and at the age of eleven, Farr made his own. After many successes with Moths and with 18-footers, and very immersed in his extreme sailboats, Farr revolutionized the long-distance yacht by designing the *45° South* for the Quarter Ton Cup in 1974. From then on, his victories were countless. In 1980, he took up with Russell Bowler, and the following year, he opened Farr Yacht Design in Annapolis, Maryland. He excelled notably in the Whitbread and then the Volvo, where he accumulated five first places between 1986 and 2002. He has participated in the Louis Vuitton Cup since its second race, always with very innovative creations, and his boats have reached the finals of the Louis Vuitton Cup three times, in 1987, 1992, and 2003. The America's Cup, however, remains his main objective.

Sir Michael Fay

In 1983, the New Zealand banker Michael Fay, born in 1949, saw the advantages in a victory in the America's Cup. He brought together the architects Bruce Farr, Russell Bowler, Ron Holland, and Laurie Davidson to create and put in the water the first 12-meter boat made of plastic, producing two hulls from the same mold. At the helm of the New Zealand, nicknamed the "Kiwi Magic," the young skipper Chris Dickson won 37 of 38 matches in the first phases of the Louis Vuitton Cup, but lost to Dennis Conner in the final.

Michael Fay then launched a rogue solo challenge at the San Diego Yacht Club in 1987, with the *New Zealand KZ 1,* dubbed the "Big Boat," 90 feet at the waterline which was decisively beaten by the catamaran *Stars & Stripes.* When the new rule was created, he entrusted the New Zealand Challenge to Bruce Farr again, and constructed four America's Cup Class boats. The New Zealand Challenge's *NZL 20* was surprisingly fast and light, but not quite fast enough to win the Louis Vuitton Cup. Fay persisted, however, and the Kiwis won the following America's Cup with the *Black Magic NZL 32,* demolishing the defender's *Young America* 5 to 0.

German Frers

Born on July 4, 1941, German Frers was a designer for fifteen years for the naval architecture firm of his father, German Frers, Sr., in Buenos Aires. At the age of seventeen, he designed the first polyester sailboat in Argentina. In 1965, Frers left for New York to work at Sparkman & Stephens, where he stayed three years before striking out on his own. On his return to Argentina in 1970, he took over his father's business. Since then, Frers has created a number of sailboats that have won all kinds of trophies, including the Admiral's Cup, the Whitbread, the Two Ton Cup, and the Maxi World.

In 1992, Raoul Gardini entrusted Frers with the design of the five *Il Moro di Venezia* boats, with which he won the IACC world championships and the Louis Vuitton Cup. As a partner with Doug Peterson in 2000, Frers created the *Luna Rossa,* another Louis Vuitton Cup winner. In 2007, His son German, Jr. ("Mani") followed in his father's footsteps; the boat he designed for the Swedish Victory Challenge, *Järv SWE 96,* made it to the finals of the 2007 Louis Vuitton Cup.

Raul Gardini

Raul Gardini announced his entry into the America's Cup one night to a group of friends dining with him in his private Venice hotel, the Ca' Dario: "This house was built sixty years before Christopher Columbus discovered America, so to me, the America's Cup is really no big deal."

Gardini launched his first Class America, *Il Moro di Venezia,* on the Grand Canal, with a display of luxury unlike anything in the history of the Cup, including the staging of a play by Franco Zeffirelli. After testing out the boat, he commissioned four more, and it was the fifth boat in this series that he brought to the Louis Vuitton Cup in 1992, with Paul Cayard at the helm. Though certain of his next victory in the America's Cup, Gardini was toppled. German Frers, upon his return from Bill Koch's hangar, where he had observed the *America³,* announced, "We have lost the Cup!"

Raoul Gardini was born in Ravenne on June 7, 1933. He began sailing very young, and built his own One Tonner, based on the plans of Dick Carter, when he was only twenty-seven. In 1976, he asked German Frers to design a Maxi for him, which marked the beginning of a lasting friendship. When a new class of sailboats was announced for the America's Cup of '92, Gardini plunged into the adventure. Only a year later, after calling to check in with each of his beloved friends, Gardini took his own life on July 23, 1993. He remains to this day an important figure in the epic history that is the America's Cup.

George "Fritz" Jewett

From 1974 to 2000, Fritz Jewett played a predominant role in American yacht racing, attracting defenders or challengers for the America's Cup. President of five syndicates, he also participated in four of Dennis Conner's campaigns with his *Stars & Stripes,* from 1987 to 1995. Then, in 2000, his last participation in the cup, he became president of the St. Francis Yacht Club challenge, Paul Cayard's *AmericaOne,* which was eliminated in the final of the Louis Vuitton Cup.

Born in 1927, Jewett graduated from Harvard in 1952 and joined the Potlatch Corporation, a forestry company. Retired from business since 1999, he was nominated in 2005 as a member of the America's Cup Hall of Fame, situated in the Herreshoff Marine Museum in Bristol, Rhode Island. He passed away on May 23, 2008.

Dyer Jones

Director of the 32nd America's Cup contest in Valencia in 2007, William H. Dyer Jones began his career in 1967, when he ran the 12-meters during the defense selections for the American defense, in Newport. At the beginning of 1974, he joined the course committee, becoming the director in 1983. Commodore of the New York Yacht Club in 1991 and 1992, he became the president of the International 12-Meter Association in 1994. After living in Valencia for three years, Jones now resides in Newport, Rhode Island, where he loves to go out with his family or friends on his 1936 Herreshoff S-boat.

Bill Koch

"Teamwork, technology, and talent. That is the approach behind the *America³.*" William "Bill" Ingraham Koch loved to quote this formula, which earned him the America's Cup in 1992 in San Diego.

Koch was born on May 3, 1940, in Wichita, Kansas, in an industrialist family. He studied at Harvard, then took a doctorate in chemistry at MIT. Later, he left the family business to create the Oxbow Group, an organization specializing in energy.

For his Maxi, the *Matador 2,* two-time world champion in 1990 and 1991, Koch developed the most important research program known today. In 1992, for the America's Cup, he surrounded himself with numerous architects, aerospace technicians, and MIT engineers to build four America's Cup Class vessels. In 1995, Koch broke new ground by financing the first crew of women in the history of the America's Cup, and their sailboat, the *Mighty Mary,* as candidates for the defense.

Ben Lexcen

Australian architect Bob Miller, known as Ben Lexcen, was born in 1936. Self-educated, he designed his first 18-footer when he was twenty-five years old. The following year, his *Venom* won the world championships.

In 1967, Miller designed *Mercedes III* for the Admiral's Cup. Following his departure from the Miller and Whitworth shipyard, he took on a pseudonym. Ben Lexcen became famous with the Admiral's Cup winners *Ginkgo* and *Apollo II,* designed for Alan Bond; then the *Southern Cross* for the America's Cup in 1974; and the *Australia* in 1977 and 1980, in collaboration with Johan Valentijn. In 1983, *Australia II* stole the America's Cup from the Americans and revolutionized sailboat design. Lexcen created three more 12-meters in 1987 and died a famous man in 1988.

Jean-Marc Loubier

Jean-Marc Loubier was born in Oran, Algeria, on October 19, 1955. After receiving his MBA from the Institut d'Etudes Politiques in Paris, he began his career as a consultant in business strategies, before joining Descamps as international director, then director of marketing and communication. In 1990, he took the same position with Louis Vuitton Malletier, with the goal of increasing Louis Vuitton's visibility in the America's Cup, making the event more accessible to the public. In 1998, he was named assistant director general. Director of Celine in the beginning of 2000, Jean-Marc quit LVMH in June 2007 to take on the directorship of the Munich-based group Escada.

Makoto Namba

Makoto Namba, the first Japanese skipper to break into the world top ten in match racing, was born on November 20, 1950, in Kyoto, the ancient imperial city. He began sailing as a student at Kyoto Sango University, and worked as a sailmaker after graduation. He was approached for the post of skipper on the Japanese America's Cup Class boat *Nippon,* although in the end it was Chris Dickson who took the helm of the sailboat in the 1992 Louis Vuitton Cup semifinals, while Makoto served as mainsail trimmer. In 1995 Namba became official skipper for the *Nippon,* which reached the Louis Vuitton Cup semifinals; his best performance was third place in the first round robin.

On the night of April 23, 1997, during a race off the coast of Osaka, Makoto Namba was swept overboard and lost at sea.

Marc Pajot

The sea air has always intoxicated Marc Pajot, who was born in La Baule, on the Atlantic coast of France, on September 21, 1953. Silver medalist with his brother Yves on the *Flying Dutchman* in the 1972 Olympics, he was a team member for Tabarly on the *Pen Duick VI* in the first Whitbread. Then he devoted himself to multihulls, with a superb victory in the Route du Rhum and a record on the *Atlantic.*

Aboard the *French Kiss* in 1987 at Fremantle, Pajot made it to the semifinals of the Louis Vuitton Cup. In San Diego in 1992, he put into the water the very first America's Cup Class boat, *FRA 1,* then the *Ville de Paris FRA 8* and *FRA 27.* Again he made it to the semifinals in the Louis Vuitton Cup, fueling hopes for future races. The *France 2* and *3* in 1995 were plagued with problems, however, and Pajot was eliminated at the end of the round robins. In Auckland, as the skipper of the eccentrically designed Swiss defender *be hAPpy,* with its two mobile-ballasted appendages, he won two out of three matches but abandoned the race after a broken mast.

The hair-raising last regatta in the 2007 race, where *Alinghi* won by one second over the *Team New Zealand,* has only whetted Pajot's desire to return . . .

Doug Peterson

Douglas Blair Peterson, born on July 25, 1945, in Los Angeles, began his career as a naval architect with a small revolution: the 1973 co–world champion of one-tonners, *Gunbare,* was surprising not only in its size but in its form. The success of Peterson's creations rapidly earned him a reputation as a leading architect; notably, he designed *Moonshine,* which won the Admiral's Cup in 1977. In 1992, Peterson was part of the important design team for defender Bill Koch's *America³,* winner of the America's Cup. On behalf of the New Zealanders, he did it again in 1995 with *Black Magic NZL 32.* Finally, for the 2000 race, he came up with the *Luna Rossa* for the Prada Challenge, Louis Vuitton Cup winners. In 2003, Peterson had a falling-out with the Prada crew during the selections and was dropped. With two Louis Vuitton Cups and two America's Cups under his belt, however, Doug Peterson remains the most prestigious designer of racing yachts of the past twenty-five years.

Henri Racamier

History started with a telephone call. In August 1982, the challengers met to begin the organization of the selection regattas. Bruno Troublé proposed to find a partnership to cover the costs of the event. And so it happened that Jean-François Bentz, the son-in-law of Henri Racamier, director of Louis Vuitton, was aboard the *France III* for a few days. They immediately called France, and two hours later, Racamier accepted: with a starting budget of $300,000, the Louis Vuitton Cup was created.

Henri Racamier was born on June 25, 1912, in Pont-en-Roide, in the Franche-Comté region of France. In 1943, he married Odile Vuitton, the daughter of Gaston-Louis Vuitton. After a career in the steel industry, he became director of Louis Vuitton in 1977. By opening individual shops selectively and modernizing the way Vuitton made and marketed its leather goods, he increased distribution while retaining the brand's exclusive cachet. In 1987, the house merged with Moët Hennessy to form LVMH, the premier luxury group in the world. Three years later, he was ousted by Bernard Arnault, whom he had invited to join LVMH in 1988.

Henri Racamier died of a heart attack in Sardinia on March 29, 2003.

Dawn Riley

The first woman to entirely direct a syndicate for the America's Cup, and having participated in three, as well as two Whitbread Round the Worlds, Dawn Riley is an accomplished sportswoman.

She was born in Detroit, by the Great Lakes. While studying at Michigan State University, she had already become captain of a sailboat crew. At the age of twenty-four, during the 1989–90 Whitbread, she was quartermaster on the *Maiden,* with an all-woman crew. Hired by Bill Koch for the defense in 1992 as pitman on the *America³,* she was the first woman to be a crew member on a winner of the America's Cup. The following year, in the Whitbread 1993–94, Riley was skipper of the *Heineken,* again with an all-woman crew. In 1995, Bill Koch named her team captain of the first all-woman crew in the history of the America's Cup, on the *Mighty Mary.* In Auckland, in 2000, she was director and skipper of the challenger *America True,* and in 2007 she was team manager of the French *K-Challenge.*

Tom Schnackenberg

Design guru Tom Schnackenberg has been on the team for three America's Cup winners: sail coordinator for *Australia II* in 1983, and design coordinator and navigator for the New Zealand "Dream Team" on *Black Magic* in 1995, and Team New Zealand in 2000. In 1977, he worked on the *Enterprise* for the defense; then, in 1980, on the challenger, the *Australia*. In 1981 and 1987, he won the Admiral's Cup.

Born on May 11, 1945, in Wellington, Schnackenberg didn't discover sailing until he was twenty-one, as a doctorate student in nuclear physics.

Schnackenberg has a reputation for innovative design, having helped develop the tri-radial genoa, 3D sails, and the famous "millennium rig" used on *Black Magic* in 2000. After the departure of Russell Coutts to the *Alinghi,* he stayed with Dean Baker and became head of the Team New Zealand syndicate in 2003. Beaten by the *Alinghi,* in 2007 he joined the *Luna Rossa* challenge team, which made it to the finals of the Louis Vuitton Cup, then worked with the Swiss to create the new America's Cup protocol.

James Spithill

"If the races were only the start and a few hundred meters, we would looking really good," James Spithill, the youngest skipper ever to sail in the America's Cup, jokingly summed up his 2000 performance on *Young Australia,* the slowest challenger. Noticed for his talent, he was recruited by Paul Cayard to train before the final of the Louis Vuitton Cup. For the America's Cup in 2003, he was hired as the helmsman by Peter Gilmour on *OneWorld USA 67,* which finished the Louis Vuitton Cup in third place.

Spithill was born in Sydney on June 28, 1979, and began match racing when he was sixteen. He was second in the Match Race World Championship in 2003, and was official world champion in 2005. Francesco de Angelis offered him the post of skipper on *Luna Rossa* for the 2007 race. He bested Chris Dickson on *BMW Oracle* 5 to 1 in the semifinals, but was beaten by Dean Barker on the *Team New Zealand* in the Louis Vuitton Cup finals. He will be part of Russell Coutts's team for the next America's Cup.

Bruno Troublé

On the eve of the fateful day, in 1983, of the seventh and final America's Cup match, Bruno Troublé took the helm of the *Challenge 12* to coach *Australia II*'s John Bertrand on starting technique, while Dennis Conner played golf. Troublé knew well the ancient dance of defense and attack, of dodge and the trap—arts learned from his grandfather and father, both members of the bar. But he turned away from law to take instead the helm of a sailboat—any sailboat would do.

Born in Versailles on May 29, 1945, Bruno Troublé followed the academic course already mapped out by his ancestors, but his dreams took him elsewhere: the sea, and the distant horizon. A dreamer but determined, he achieved his dream: he became skipper on Marcel Bich's boats *France 1* and *France 2,* reaching the 1977 and 1980 America's Cup finals, then on the *France 3* in 1983. In 1983, with Henri Racamier, Troublé founded the Louis Vuitton Cup, becoming the cup's guiding spirit and its essential organizer.

Twice in the Olympics, many times world champion, Troublé continues to race yachts and has been elected into the America's Cup Hall of Fame.

Rolf Vrolijk

"Go narrow," was the thinking of the Dutch yacht architect Rolf Vrolijk before the 2000 America's Cup. "Generally, you want to be as narrow as possible. But there is a limit—and trying to catch that limit is the interesting part . . . " Vrolijk has pushed the limit to good effect: his boats have twice won the America's Cup, in 2003 and 2007.

Born on Christmas Day in 1946, Vrolijk has always been a sailor. Becoming a naval architect, for him, was inevitable. A mechanical engineer, in 1978, he teamed up with Friedrich Judel to found Judel-Vrolijk, which quickly became one of the most important yacht design firms in Europe. His *Bravo España ESP 47,* came in eighth in the Louis Vuitton Cup in 2000, but Bertrand Pacé, the French skipper, considered the Spanish boat to be the best 2000 design on the water. Vrolijk also completely redesigned the *Rioja de España ESP 42,* transforming it into the *Bravo España ESP 56.*

As manager of the design team for the *Alinghi,* Vrolijk designed the challenger victor of the Louis Vuitton Cup and the America's Cup in 2003, and then the triumphant defender in 2007.

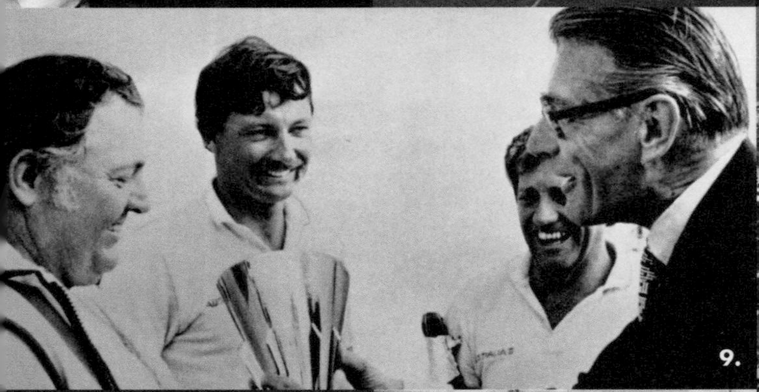

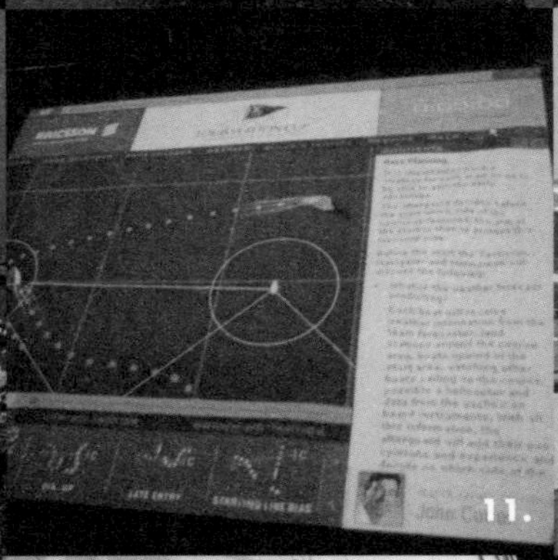

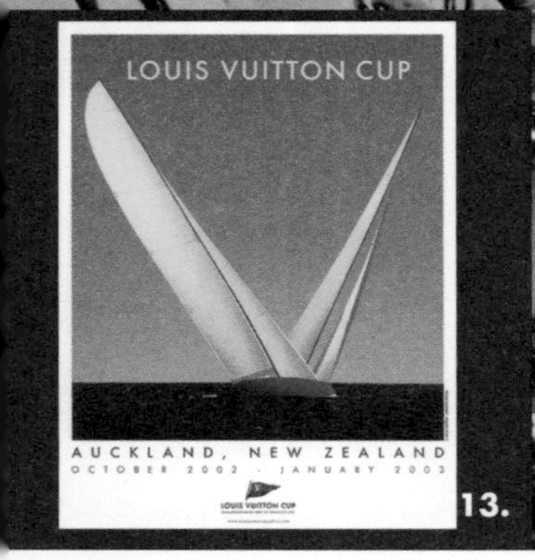

1. The Louis Vuitton Media Center in Auckland in the Maritime Museum held more than 1,000 journalists in 2003. Here, a new section dedicated to Sir Peter Blake will open soon.
© Archives Louis Vuitton / Antoine Jarrier

2. Laurent Korcia and his Stradivarius during the party organized by the Civic Theatre of Auckland in 2000.
© Archives Louis Vuitton / Antoine Jarrier

3. Paul Cayard holds up the Louis Vuitton Cup beside Yves Carcelle in the San Diego press center at the end of the last press conference in 1992.
© Bob Grieser

4. President Bill Clinton, here accompanied by Mélanie and Bruno Troublé, came to Auckland in 2000 to participate in the APEC conference.
© Bruce Jarvis

5. In Auckland in 2003, a village was organized around the port. Of the just under four million New Zealanders, more than a million and a half came to see the races.
© Archives Louis Vuitton / Antoine Jarrier

6 . A grand parade down the streets of Auckland marks the commencement of the Louis Vuitton Cup in October 1999.
© Archives Louis Vuitton / Antoine Jarrier

7. Christine Bélanger, who is responsible for the grand events hosted by Louis Vuitton, knows the Cup very well. Present with Moët & Chandon for the 1986 contest in Australia, she has not missed a single race since.
© Archives Louis Vuitton / Luca Villata

8. Fremantle remains in everyone's memory—a new land of wind, sun, and magnificent regattas. On the last day, photographers swarmed onto fishing boats to welcome Dennis Conner's *Stars & Stripes*.
© Philip Plisson / Pêcheur d'Images.

9. Henry Racamier hands the Louis Vuitton Cup over to the winners during the first competition in 1983. From left to right: Alan Bond, John Bertrand, Warren Jones, and Henry Racamier.
© Archives Louis Vuitton

10. New Zealand may have lost the Cup in 2003, but the city of Auckland profited by the focus on its port, and the country enjoyed immense visibility around the globe.
© Gilles Martin-Raget

11. Since 1995, Louis Vuitton has taken the initiative to broadcast directly from the regattas, using computer-generated images.
© Archives Louis Vuitton / Antoine Jarrier

12. The Luna Rossa's base in Valencia, designed by Renzo Piano, certainly earned the architecture prize in 2007. The hangar structure is covered in cloth.
© Luca Villata

13. The French artist Razzia has created all of the posters for the Louis Vuitton Cup since 1987. These colorful illustrations make the most of the special light at each of the ports where the tests were organized.
© Archives Louis Vuitton / Razzia

14. New Zealand hero Sir Edmund Hillary and Maori dancers livened up the ceremonies in 2003. Here is the closing show.
© François Chevalier

15. The main room of the press center in Auckland allowed those watching to see all the regattas simultaneously. The journalists here could follow the regattas better here than those on the water!
© Collection Bruno Troublé

16. Fremantle 1987: Dennis Conner returns to port victorious, having avenged his historic defeat in 1983. Here, he welcomes supporters on board to join his celebration.
© Collection Bruno Troublé

17. The program for the first Louis Vuitton Cup in 1983 in Newport, Rhode Island.
© Creative Business/Collection Bruno Troublé

18. The port of Auckland in 2003.
© Gilles Martin-Raget

19. The party organized in 1992 on the American nuclear aircraft carrier *USS Kitty Hawk* was one for the history books! The boat had just come from the Gulf War, and all the equipment and planes were still on board. The guests were even allowed to sit in the cockpits of the fighter planes!
© Merpool

20. Bill Clinton, like other presidents before him, came to follow the American teams. Here, with his daughter, Chelsea, he cheers on the Hawaiian boat, the *Abracadabra*, in 2000.
© Archives Louis Vuitton/Richard Simpson

21. The 2007 Louis Vuitton party at La Cartuja, in Valencia. In a performance created by Alfio Pozzoni, two gymnasts pretend to fight for the Cup in an aquarium.
© Bob Grieser

22. A Mexican party in San Diego in 1992 to celebrate the Italian victory!
© Archives Louis Vuitton/Kaoru Soehata

23. The drawing of lots for the Louis Vuitton Cup in 1995, broadcast live by CBS.
© Archives Louis Vuitton/Daniel Forster

24. A moving image of Dean Barker and Russell Coutts, after their successful defense of the America's Cup in Auckland in 2000.
© François Mousis

25. Raul Gardini and Jean-Marc Loubier pass through an honor guard created for the 1992 Louis Vuitton Cup in San Diego.
© Louis Vuitton Media Center

26. In 1987, Louis Vuitton created an Epi leather transport case for the America's Cup. It was later remade in the company's signature Monogram Canvas.
© Archives Louis Vuitton

27 . Sir Peter Blake and one of his teammates land right in the middle of the guests during the Luis Vuitton Top Gun party of 1995—the only party attended by the New Zealand team, who were concentrating only on winning!
© Archives Louis Vuitton

28. The Civic Theatre of Auckland, reopened for the occasion, hosted the Louis Vuitton Cup in 1999.
© Collection Bruno Troublé

29. Lapo Elkan, Antoine Arnault, and Pietro Beccari, director of publicity for Louis Vuitton, in Valencia in 2007.
© Archives Louis Vuitton/Bob Grieser

30. Bruno Troublé at the helm of the *France III* in 1980. The baron stays close at hand to keep an eye on what happens on board, ready to take the helm himself if the regatta is lost, or if his boat wins!
© Collection Bruno Troublé

31. With the city's cooperation, the streets of San Diego are decorated with the colors of the Louis Vuitton Cup and the America's Cup.
© Christian Février

32. Ted Turner did not just create CNN! The American businessman, here at the helm of the *Endeavour,* is an exceptional sailor. As skipper of the *Courageous* in 1977, he won the America's Cup.
© Collection Bruno Troublé

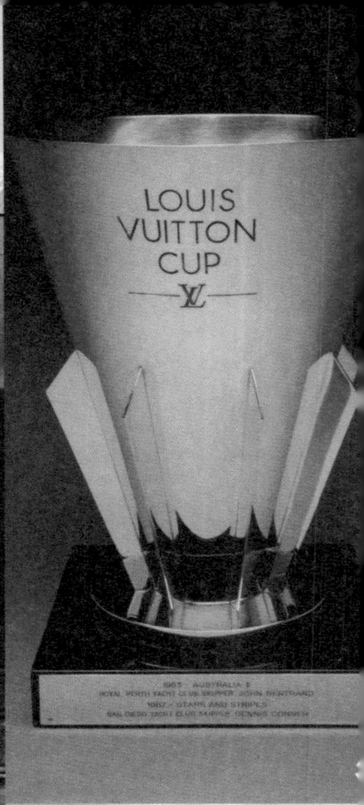

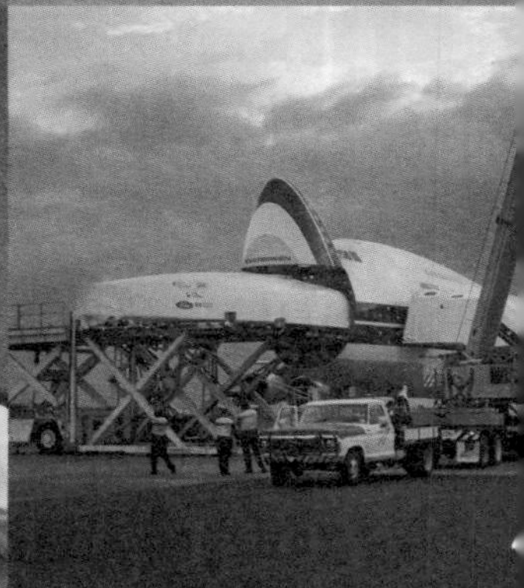

33. Dennis Conner receives the Louis Vuitton Cup in 1987 from the hands of Henri Racamier, a few days before coming back to pick up his bonus: the America's Cup!
© Collection Bruno Troublé

34. The awards dinner of 2007: a table nearly 400 feet long is set up in the conservatory of the Umbracle gardens, created by Santiago Calatrava.
© Archives Louis Vuitton

35. Watch out for pirates! Carlo Borlenghi and Marcus Hutchinson lie in wait for competitors on board the giant buoy in Malmö in 2006.
© Collection Bruno Troublé

36. Amateur sailor in his leisure time, Yves Carcelle had his chance to participate in a regatta on the Spanish boat, semifinalist in the 2007 Louis Vuitton Cup.
© Marina Könitzer

37. The outcome of many regattas is uncertain until the very end. Here, in Auckland in 2000, the press room team is glued to the monitor as only six feet separate the boats on their approach to the finish line.
© Collection Bruno Troublé

38. The Valencia Opera, built by Santiago Calatrava, decorated with the Louis Vuitton colors during the last day of the 2007 regattas.
© Luca Villata

39. The Louis Vuitton Cup: an old design by the Parisian silversmith Jean Puiforcat, re-created for the occasion in November 1982, and passed from winner to winner from 1983 to 2007.
© Archives Louis Vuitton

40. The Foredeck, designed by the British architect David Chipperfield, makes a spectacular lookout over the entrance of the port of Valencia in 2007.
© Collection Bruno Troublé

41. The New Zealanders in triumph! They won the Louis Vuitton Cup, and made it to the ultimate duel against the Swiss *Alinghi*.
© Bob Grieser

42. To gain time, these enormous Russian planes—the only ones large enough—take boats from one continent to another.
© Gilles Martin-Raget

43. To mark his neutrality toward the two finalists of 1987, New Zealand and America, at a press conference, Bruno Troublé sports a shirt with the colors of both countries!
© Christian Février

44. The all-woman team of the *Mighty Mary* makes its mark in 1995!
© Gilles Martin-Raget

45. Captain Salvatore Sarno. This man made possible South Africa's remarkable entrance to the most publicized sailing event in the world.
© Collection Bruno Troublé

46. During training sessions, Baron Bich often takes the helm in his white linen jacket!
© Erwan Quéméré

47. In the long quarrel between the Italians and the New Zealanders during the final of the Louis Vuitton Cup in 1992, Bruce Farr defends the Kiwi team's use of the bowsprit before an international jury.
© Gilles Martin-Raget

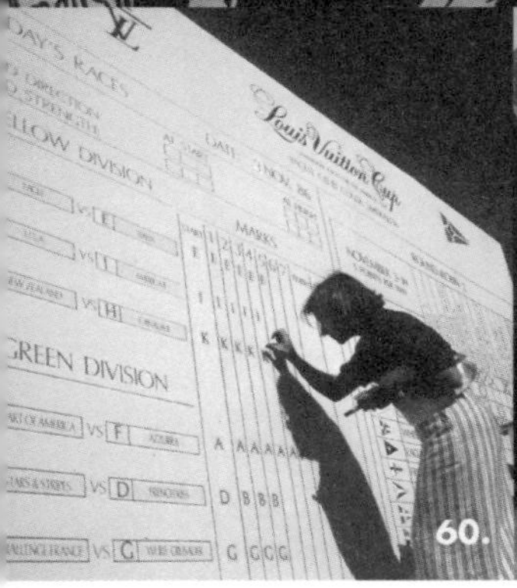

48. The organization team of the Louis Vuitton Cup at the Yacht Club Costa Smeralda in 1986.
© Collection Bruno Troublé

49. Alan Bond and Commodore Stan Reid receive the America's Cup in 1983.
© Christian Février

50. Lady Diana, who has come to christen the English boat in 1986, is welcomed by the representatives of Louis Vuitton.
© Collection Bruno Troublé

51. In the Louis Vuitton Act 1 in Marseille in September 2004, children parade down the Canebière with the Cup.
© Collection Bruno Troublé

52. Antoine Arnault and Yves Carcelle during the launch party given by the Emirates Team New Zealand in Valencia in 2007.
© Collection Bruno Troublé

53. The ultramodern port built especially for the event by the Spanish makes an extraordinary setting for the 32nd America's Cup in Valencia.
© Gilles Martin-Raget

54. Yves Carcelle in 2006 with the two trophies that he carried in his luggage on a trip to China to promote the race.
© Collection Bruno Troublé

55. Baron Marcel Bich with Poppy Delfour and Bruno Troublé after their last race in 1980—the best French result to this day.
© Collection Bruno Troublé

56. The "Lion of Venice": Raul Gardini, winner of the 1992 Louis Vuitton Cup in San Diego.
© Collection Bruno Troublé

57. A dramatic spectacle at the Louis Vuitton party in 2003 on the dry dock at Devonport, New Zealand.
© Kaoru Soehata

58. The enormous buoy created for the 2007 Louis Vuitton Acts put cameramen and photographers at the heart of the action.
© Bob Grieser

59. Captain Dyer Jones with Walter and Betsy Cronkite in 1987 in Fremantle.
© Bruno Troublé

60. Scoreboards giving up-to-date information as each buoy was passed allowed the public to follow the regattas.
© Gilles Martin-Raget

61. Captain Nicholson and Yves Carcelle cement the famous bollard before the Royal Yacht Squadron at Cowes. A gift by Louis Vuitton and designed by Gregory Ryan, the bollard celebrates 150 years of the America's Cup.
© Archives Louis Vuitton/Jon Nash

62. Through the years, the Louis Vuitton organization team has multiplied! There are around 210 team members in this picture taken in 2000 in Auckland.
© Archives Louis Vuitton/Gilles Martin-Raget

63. Jacques Chirac, then mayor of Paris, accompanies skipper Marc Pajot on the *Ville de Paris* in San Diego, 1992.
© Collection Bruno Troublé

LOUIS VUITTON CUP 1983–2007

Statistics Summay

Year	*Winner*	*Yacht Club*	*Country*	*Skipper*	*Challenger*	*Yacht Club*	*Country*	*Skipper*	*Results*	*Location*
1983	*Australia II* *KA 6*	Royal Perth Yacht Club	Australia	John Bertrand	*Victory 83* *K 22*	Royal Burnham Yacht Club	United Kingdom	Harold Cudmore	4 – 1	Newport, Rhode Island
1987	*Stars & Stripes* *US 55*	San Diego Yacht Club	United States	Dennis Conner	*New Zealand* *KZ 7*	Royal New Zealand Yacht Squadron	New Zealand	Chris Dickson	4 – 1	Fremantle, Australia
1992	*Il Moro di Venezia V* *ITA 25*	Compagnia della Vela	Italy	Paul Cayard	*New Zealand* *NZL 20*	Mercury Bay Boating Club	New Zealand	Rod Davis	5 – 3	San Diego, California
1995	*Black Magic* *NZL 32*	Royal New Zealand Yacht Squadron	New Zealand	Peter Blake Russell Coutts	*oneAustralia* *AUS 35*	Southern Cross Yacht Club	Australia	Rod Davis	5 – 1	San Diego, California
2000	*Luna Rossa* *ITA 45*	Yacht Club Punta Ala	Italy	Francesco de Angelis	*AmericaOne* *USA 61*	St Francis Yacht Club	United States	Paul Cayard	5 – 4	Auckland, New Zealand
2003	*Alinghi* *SUI 64*	Société Nautique de Genève	Switzer-land	Russell Coutts	*Oracle BMW* *USA 76*	Golden Gate Yacht Club	United States	Peter Holmberg	5 – 1	Auckland, New Zealand
2007	*Team New Zealand* *NZL 92*	Royal New Zealand Yacht Squadron	New Zealand	Dean Barker	*Luna Rossa* *ITA 94*	Yacht Club Italiano	Italy	Francesco de Angelis James Spithill	5 – 0	Valencia, Spain

AMERICA'S CUP 1983–2007

Statistics Summary

Year	*Winner*	*Yacht Club*	*Country*	*Skipper*	*Challenger*	*Yacht Club*	*Country*	*Skipper*	*Results*	*Location*
1983	*Australia II* *KA 6*	Royal Perth Yacht Club	Australia	John Bertrand	*Liberty* *US 40*	New York Yacht Club	United States	Dennis Conner	4 – 3	Newport, Rhode Island
1987	*Stars & Stripes* *USA 55*	San Diego Yacht Club	United States	Dennis Conner	*Kookaburra III* *KA 15*	Royal Perth Yacht Club	Australia	Iain Murray	4 – 0	Fremantle, Australia
1988	*Stars & Stripes* *USA 1*	San Diego Yacht Club	United States	Dennis Conner	*New Zealand* *KZ 1*	Mercury Bay Boating Club	New Zealand	David Barnes	2 – 0	San Diego, California
1992	*America^3* *USA 23*	San Diego Yacht Club	United States	Bill Koch Buddy Melge	*Il Moro di Venezia V* *ITA 25*	Compagnia della Vela	Italy	Paul Cayard	4 – 1	San Diego, California
1995	*Black Magic* *NZL 32*	Royal New Zealand Yacht Squadron	New Zealand	Peter Blake Russell Coutts	*Young America* *USA 36*	New York Yacht Club	United States	Dennis Conner	5 – 0	San Diego, California
2000	*Team New Zealand* *NZL 60*	Royal New Zealand Yacht Squadron	New Zealand	Russell Coutts Dean Barker	*Luna Rossa* *ITA 45*	Yacht Club Punta Ala	Italy	Francesco de Angelis	5 – 0	Auckland, New Zealand
2003	*Alinghi* *SUI 64*	Société Nautique de Genève	Switzer-land	Russell Coutts	*Team New Zealand* *NZL 82*	Royal New Zealand Yacht Squadron	New Zealand	Dean Barker	5 – 0	Auckland, New Zealand
2007	*Alinghi* *SUI 100*	Société Nautique de Genève	Switzer-land	Brad Butterworth Ed Baird	*Team New Zealand* *NZL 92*	Royal New Zealand Yacht Squadron	New Zealand	Dean Barker	5 – 2	Valencia, Spain

GLOSSARY

Abeam. Point of sail with the wind at right angles to the boat.
Acts. A series of qualifying fleet and match races held between 2004 and 2007 between the challengers and the defender, earning bonus points that will carry over to the Louis Vuitton Cup.
Aground. When the hull or the keel is against the ground.
America's Cup. An international regatta dating back to 1851; cup given to the winner of the America's Cup, designed and built in 1848 by Robert Garrard, the Royal Jeweller of England. Originally the One Hundred Guineas Cup, it was renamed the America's Cup when the yacht *America* won it in 1851.
Back stay. A cable supporting the mast, usually running from the stern to the head of the mast; part of the standing rigging.
Ballast. Weight in the keel of the boat to add stability.
Battens. Flexible wooden or plastic strips fitted into pockets to stiffen a sail.
Beam. Widest part of a boat.
Bear away. Steer the boat away from the wind.
Beaufort scale. Created in 1806 by the Irish-British admiral Sir Francis Beaufort (1774–1857), the Beaufort scale ranks wind strength from 0 to 12. Each number corresponds to a condition of the sea. Force 8, between 34 and 40 knots of wind, signifies a "fresh gale"; Force 10, a storm; and Force 12, above 64 knots, a hurricane.
Bermudan rig. A triangular mainsail, without an upper spar, which is hoisted up the mast by a single halyard attached to the head of the sail.
Boom. Spar at right angles to the mast that holds the foot of a sail.
Bosun's chair. A seat, usually made of canvas, used to hoist a person up the mast.
Bow. The front of the boat.
Bowsprit. Spar extending forward from the bow of a sailboat.
Bulb. The lead-torpedo shape on the bottom of the keel.
Buried bow. When a boat runs into a wave, and water covers the foredeck.
Catamaran. Boat with two hulls.
Chainplates. Metal plates bolted to the boat to which standing rigging is attached.
Challenger. A yacht club whose challenge has been accepted by the America's Cup defender and includes a person or entity that undertakes that yacht club's challenge as its representative.
Challenger of Record. The yacht club whose challenge has been accepted by the defender yacht club under the terms of the Deed of Gift for the America's Cup and whose challenge is current.
Circling. Tactical maneuver that consists of sailing in tight circles to maneuver for a favorable position at the start of a match race.
Clipper. A fast, elegant transoceanic sailing vessel with three or four tall masts.
Close-hauled. Point of sail at which the boat is heading as close to the wind as it can without starting to luff.
Coaster. Single-masted vessel with at least two foresails, a jib and a staysail.
Cockpit. The somewhat protected area below deck level from which the tiller or wheel is handled.
Cordage. The nautical term for all ropes on a boat, apart from that used to pull the bell, the only rope on the boat that is called a rope.
Deck. Horizontal surface or platform of a yacht.
Deck equipment. All of the equipment used on deck for maneuvering, navigation, and safety, such as winches, cleats, blocks, compasses, and stanchions.
Deed of Gift. The primary document that governs the rules for entering and participating in the America's Cup, originally forwarded by George L. Schuyler to the New York Yacht Club on July 8, 1887.
Defender. The yacht club holding the America's Cup and that includes a person or entity that undertakes that yacht club's defense as its representative.
Design rule. The formulas and calculations used to define a class of boats or establish a handicap to make the chances of winning as close as possible for different boats.
Displacement. The weight of the water displaced by a yacht.
Downwind. With the wind coming from behind.
Draft. Distance between the water level and the lowest point of a yacht.
Floating dock. A platform supported by a floating device where boats can be moored.
Foot. The bottom edge of a sail.
Freeboard. Distance from the water to the top edge of the hull.
Frigate. Three-masted war vessel, smaller than a ship.
Furl. To roll up and bind a sail on its yard or boom.
Genoa. A large foresail, larger than a jib, that overlaps the mainsail.
Half-hull. Scale model representing the starboard side of a boat's hull.
Halyard. A line used to raise and lower the sails; part of the running rigging.
Heel. The leeward lean of the boat, caused by the wind's pressure on the sail.
IACC. International America's Cup Class, created specially in 1992 for the America's Cup.
International Rule. Adopted in 1906 in London by European yachters, ratified in 1907, and modified in 1917 and 1933, the International Rule was created to measure and rate yachts so that craft of different design could race together under a handicap system. The formula, which is expressed in meters, is based on waterline length, chain girth, sail area, and the difference in chain and girth.
International 12-meter class. A group of sailing vessels designed to a particular formula, according to the International Rule. The first 12-meter boat was built in 1907; the 12-meter class was the standard for the America's Cup between 1958 and 1987.
J-class. Class of boat defined by the Universal Rule used in the America's Cup between 1930 and 1937.
Jib. Triangular sail in front of the mast. Large sailing vessels may have four jibs: the fore staysail, the inner jib, the outer jib, and the flying jib.
Jibe. To change tack while going downwind. A difficult maneuver in a strong wind.
Keel. A ballasted projection below the boat that keeps it from capsizing, and supplies the hydrodynamic lateral force that enables the boat to sail upwind.
Knot. Unit of speed measured in nautical miles per hour.
Leeward. Side away from the direction of the wind.
Louis Vuitton Cup. Series of regattas to select the challenger for the America's Cup; cup given to the winner of the Louis Vuitton Cup, designed by the Parisian goldsmith Jean Puiforcat.
Luff. To change course toward the wind.
Match race. A boat race in which only two yachts, usually similar or in the same class, compete at a time, as opposed to "fleet racing," where more yachts sail at once.
Maxi. A boat designed to the maximum rating allowed under the International Offshore Rule, or more recently, the international measurement system.
Monohull. Boat with only one hull.
Multihull. A vessel with two or three hulls.
Nautical mile. Unit of distance on the sea, equal to one minute of latitude; approximately 6,076 feet, or 1.15 miles.
Planking. The boards or metal that make up the skin.
Point of sail. Positions of a boat relative to the wind. At a close-hauled point of sail, the boat is heading as close to the wind as it can without starting to luff; at a running point of sail, the wind is coming from directly behind the boat.
Port. The left side of the boat.
Rating. Result of the calculations given in the design rule, allowing a boat to be assigned to a particular class or a handicap to be calculated to level the chances of winning for different boats.
Repechage. A trial heat in which first-round losers are given another chance to qualify for the semifinals.
Rigging. The standing rigging comprises the mast and its support lines; running rigging, the lines used to adjust the sails.

Round robin. Series of races between two boats in which each of the challengers or defenders can meet one or more times, each victory being awared a certain number of points.
Rudder cables. Cables attaching the rudder to the **tiller**.
Rudder head. The underwater portion of the rudder.
Running. **Point of sail** with the wind coming from behind.
Running backstay. An adjustable cable running from the top of the mast to the stern of the boat.
Schooner. Two-masted vessel with a foremast and a mainmast nearly amidships.
Sheet. A line used to control a sail; part of the **running rigging**. One **trims** or **slacks** a sheet.
Shrouds. Support cables for the mast; part of the standing **rigging**.
Sister ship. A way of describing vessels built according to the same design plan.
Skin. The outer envelope of a boat, composed of **planking**.
Skipper. The person in charge of a yacht.
Slack. To loosen **sheet** or **cordage**.
Spar. Any pole in the **rigging** of a boat, such as the mast, yard, or **boom**.
Spinnaker. A large ballooning sail that is flown in front of the yacht when the wind comes from aft of **abeam**.
Spinnaker pole. A pole that is attached to the lower front of the mast to hold one corner of a **spinnaker** out from the yacht.
Spreaders. Short horizontal struts extending from the mast to the sides of the boat, changing the upward angle of the **shrouds**.
Starboard. The right side of a boat.
Stays. Lines that support a mast, running from near the top of the mast to the **bow** and to both sides of the hull; part of the standing **rigging**.
Staysail. A small sail flown between the mast and the inner forestay.
Tack (noun). A **point of sail** with the wind on one side of the boat; on a **starboard** tack the wind comes from the right; on a **port** tack it comes from the left.
Tack (verb). To turn the **bow** of the yacht toward the wind, changing the sides of the sails; by extension, to change direction often and sail on a zigzag course.
Tiller. The bar or wheel the helmsman holds to control the rudder.
Trade winds. Relatively constant winds in the Atlantic that blow toward the equator.
Trim (noun). Fore-and-aft balance of a boat in relation to the waterline.
Trim (verb). To adjust a sail by pulling on a **sheet** or a rope.
Universal Rule. Created in 1903 by American architect Nathanael Herreshoff, this rule used a formula based on boat length, sail area, and displacement to classify vessels: **schooners** were assigned to classes A through F; **sloops**, to classes G through R. The **J-class** yachts used in the **America's Cup** were rated from 65 to 76 feet.
Upwind. Into the wind.
Weight estimate. A figure estimating the weight of all the parts of a yacht, used to calculate its displacement.
Winch. A cylindrical device used to give a mechanical advantage when **trimming** or **slacking** the sails on the lines.
Winch pedestal. An upright **winch** drive mechanism with two handles to increase purchasing power.
Windward. Side from which the wind is coming.

ACKNOWLEDGMENTS

Thanks to: Daniel Allisy, Isabelle Andrieux, Sébastien Beauvilain, Beken of Cowes Library, Sophie Berteloot, Pierre-Marie Bourguinat, Arielle Cassim, Laurent Charpentier, Alice Chevalier, Brigitte Chevalier-Brest, Christian Février, Daniel Forster, Dominique Gabirault, Bob Grieser, Guy Gurney, Hervé Hillard, Michèle Hors, Marcus Hutchinson, Bruce Jarvis, Könitzer, Arnaud Letrésor at DPPI, Gilles Martin-Raget, Anne Mensior, Alain Mousis, Mystic Seaport Museum, Jon Nash, New York Yacht Club, Bernard Nivelt, Marc Pajot, Doug Peterson, Valentine Petit, Philip and Guillaume Plisson and the team at Pêcheurs d'image, Fabienne Ploquin, Erwan Quéméré, Philippe Quentin, Razzia, Didier Ravon, Antoine Ricardoux, Florence Richin, Guy Roland-Perrin, Royal Yacht Squadron, Antoine Sezerat, Frank Socha, Kaoru Soehata, Olin J. Stephens, Mélanie Troublé, Maguelonne Turcat, Margot Verneuil, Luca Villata, Richard Walch, and Louisa Watrous at Mariner's Museum.

Thanks to the whole team at Maison Louis Vuitton, and particularly to Christine Bélanger, Elise Bracq, Yves Carcelle, François Dessault, Marie-Laure Fourt, Isabelle Franchet, Julien Guerrier, Antoine Jarrier, Florence Lesché, Nathalie Moullé-Berteaux, and Mazen Saggar.

BIBLIOGRAPHY

Alinghi. Lausanne, France: Favre, 2007.

Bonnet, Pierre F., and Eugène-Louis Dumont. *Société Nautique de Genève: Cent ans d'histoire, 1872–1972.* Geneva: S.N.G., n.d.

Boyd, Jeff, and Doug Hunter. *Trials "Canada 1" and the 1983 America's Cup.* Toronto: Macmillan of Canada, 1984.

Center, Bill. *America's Cup '95: The Official Record, the Louis Vuitton Cup, the Citizen Cup, the America's Cup.* Del Mar, Calif.: Tehabi, 1995.

Chevalier, François, and Jacques Taglang. *America's Cup Yacht Designs, 1851–1986.* Paris: privately printed, 1987.

Clark, Mark. *Red Dog and Great White: Inside the America's Cup.* New York: Byren House, 1986.

Coat, Tom. *A Cup of Controversy: The Intrigue Behind the Strangest America's Cup Ever.* Privately printed, 1988.

Cole, Mervyn C. *The America's Cup Cartoon Collection, from Newspapers Around the World.* South Perth, Australia: Kara International, 1984.

Conner, Dennis, and Bruce Stannard. *Comeback: My Race for the America's Cup.* New York: St. Martins Press, 1987.

Conner, Dennis, and John Rousmaniere. *No Excuse to Lose: Winning the Races.* New York: W. W. Norton, 1987.

Coutts, Russell, and Paul C. Larsen. *Challenge 2000: The Race to Win the America's Cup.* Alexandria, Va.: Time Life, 1999.

Fairchild, Tony. *America's Cup Challenge: There Is No Second.* London: Macmillan Nautical Books, 1983.

Fisher, Henry. *Absorbing Interest: The America's Cup, A History, 1851–2003.* London: Fernhurst, 2007.

Freer, Chris. *The Twelve-Metre Yacht: Its Evolution and Design, 1906–1987.* London: Nautical Books, 1986.

Gilles, Daniel. *La Coupe de l'America: Cent Quarante et un ans de régates pour un pichet d'argent.* Paris: Gallimard, 1992.

Johnson, Peter. *Yacht Rating.* New York: John Wiley and Sons, 1997.

Lang, Luigi, and Dyer Jones. *The 12 Metre Class: The History of The International 12 Metre Class from the First International Rule to the America's Cup.* London: Adlar Coles Nautical, London, 2001.

Larsen, Paul C. *To the Third Power: The Inside Story of Bill Koch's Winning Strategies for the America's Cup.* Gardiner, Maine: Tilbury House, 1995.

———. *Russell Coutts: Course to Victory.* Auckland, New Zealand: Hodder Moa Beckett, 1996.

Levitt, Michael. *America's Cup, 1851 to 1992: The Official Record of America's Cup XXVIII and the Louis Vuitton Cup.* Portland, Oregon: Portland Graphic Arts Center, 1992.

Levitt, Michael, and Barbara Lloyd. *Upset: Australia Wins the America's Cup.* New York: Workman, 1983.

Morgan, Adrian, Tim Jeffery, Stuart Alexander, Chris Freer, and Barry Pickthall. *America's Cup '87: Sail of the Century.* New York: Sheridan House, 1987.

Noverraz, Oliver. *Coupe de l'America 2003: Le Fabuleux Défi Suisse.* Le Touvet, France: Éditions Marcel-Didier Vrac, 2003.

Ottone, Piero. *Dall' "America" all' "Azzurra," 1851–1983.* Milan: Gruppo Editoriale Fabri, 1983.

Pajot, Marc, and Thierry Rannou. *Défi à la Coupe de l'America.* Paris: Rivages-Les Échos, 1987.

Parkinson, John, Jr. *The History of the New York Yacht Club, from its Founding through 1973.* New York: NYYC, 1975.

Pasols, Paul-Gérard. *Louis Vuitton: La Naissance du luxe moderne.* Paris: Éditions de La Martinière, 2005.

Pèrètiè, Olivier. *Coupe de l'America 87: La Revanche aux Antipodes.* Paris: Hachette, 1987.

Riggs, Doug. *Keelhauled, Unsportsmanlike Conduct and the America's Cup.* Newport, Rhode Island: Seven Seas Press, 1986.

Rousmaniere, John. *America-Australia, 1851–1983: Histoire d'une régate de cent trente deux ans.* Paris: Gallimard, 1983.

Seaton Huntington, Anna. *Making Waves: The Inside Story of Managing and Motivating the First Women's Team to Compete for the America's Cup.* Irving, Texas: Summit, 1996.

Sefton, Alan. *The Cup Down Under: The America's Cup 1987.* Stamford, Conn.: Longmeadow Press, 1987.

Smith, Patrick. *The Nippon Challenge: Japan's Pursuit of the America's Cup.* New York: Doubleday, 1995.

Stannard, Bruce. *"Australia II": The Official Record.* Sydney: Joyce Childress Management, 1984.

———. *Ben Lexcen: The Man, the Keel and the Cup.* London: Faber & Faber, 1984.

———. *"Stars & Stripes": The Official Record.* San Diego: Dennis Conner, 1988.

———. *The Triumph of "Australie II."* Sydney: Lansdowne, 1983.

Thompson, Winfield M., William P. Stephens, and William U. Swan. *The Yacht "America."* Boston: Charles E. Lauriat, 1925.

Vaughan, Roger. *America's Cup XXVII, "Stars & Stripes": The Official Record, 1988.* San Diego, Calif.: Dennis Conner, 1988.

Wheatley, Keith. *America's Cup '87: The Inside Story.* London: Michael Joseph, 1986.

Wilkins, Ivor. *Quest for the Cup, "BMW Oracle" Racing: The Journey Begins, 2003–2005.* Auckland, New Zealand: Oracle Racing, 2005.

Magazines

The America's Cup Louis Vuitton Newsletter
Countdown to Perth '87
Course au Large
Cuplegend
Kazi
L'Equipe Magazine
Mainsail
Mer & Bateaux
Nautical Quarterly
Régates International
Sail
Seahorse
Vela
Voiles & Voiliers
Yachting
Yachting World

For each challenge: Protocols governing the Louis Vuitton Cup, sailing instructions, official programs, and race results issued by the America's Cup Louis Vuitton Media Center, and the publications and press packs on the challengers and the defenders.

INDEX

Page numbers in italics refer to photographs or drawings